ON DOING GOOD

❖ GERALD JONAS ❖

CHARLES SCRIBNER'S SONS ❖ NEW YORK

To SUSAN

ACKNOWLEDGMENTS

As will be clear to any reader, the historical sections of this book draw extensively on the research and writings of Francis Paul Jennings, who is currently chairman of the history department at Cedar Crest College, Allentown, Pennsylvania. I found especially useful his detailed study, *Miquon's Passing: Indian-European Relations in Colonial Pennsylvania, 1674 to 1755* (1965). In addition, Professor Jennings welcomed me into his home for an invaluable briefing on the intricacies of this early and sadly prophetic conflict along the racial and cultural frontiers of North America. The use I have made of this material is entirely my own, and Professor Jennings bears no responsibility for any errors of fact or interpretation.

My debt to the many people connected with the American Friends Service Committee who answered my questions and shared their experiences with me should also be clear. At all times I was given full cooperation, and a completely free hand. But I am pleased to take this opportunity to express my special thanks to Margaret Bacon of the Committee's public relations staff. An author and historian in her own right, she acted as my guide on my innumerable visits to Philadelphia, and in every way led me to a broader and deeper understanding of the inexhaustible subject which I have attempted to treat from one limited perspective in this book.

CONTENTS

Interest in the common good is at present so weak a motive in the generality, not because it can never be otherwise, but because the mind is not accustomed to dwell on it as it dwells from morning till night on things which tend only to personal advantage.... The deep-rooted selfishness, which forms the general character of the existing state of society, is so deeply rooted only because the whole course of existing institutions tends to foster it; and modern institutions in some respects more than ancient....

—JOHN STUART MILL,
Autobiography (1873)

Your liberals and radicals all want to govern. They want to try it their way—to show that people will be happier if the power is wielded in a different way or for different purposes. But how do they know? Have they ever tried it? No, it's merely their guess.

—B. F. SKINNER
Walden Two (1948)

ON DOING GOOD

THE
ARGUMENT

❖ ❖ ❖

NOBODY loves a do-gooder. The word itself irritates people. *Webster's Third International Dictionary* gives only one meaning for "do-gooder": "An earnest usu. impractical-minded humanitarian bent on promoting welfare work or reform—commonly used with a derogatory implication of naivete or blundering ineffectualness." Two other recently compiled lexicons (*American Heritage* and *Random House*) make the point even more strongly; they conjure up an army of self-righteous busybodies intent on reshaping society in their own image. The image is all too familiar, and it is hardly surprising that society should take linguistic revenge on such highly visible but essentially powerless troublemakers. More significant, perhaps, is the lack of a corresponding, nonpejorative idiom—a word or phrase in current English usage to describe the person who devotes himself to practical, efficient labors on behalf of a better world. Do we really believe that no such people exist? Or does our language mirror the self-doubts we feel in their presence? We have no difficulty identifying isolated acts of an "altruistic" nature, and we can talk freely about the abstract concept of "altruism" —"uncalculated consideration of others' interests." Yet we would feel foolish in labeling anyone a full-time altruist. "Philanthropist" (from the Greek for "loving" and "man") might have served once, but over the years it has acquired a limiting connotation of economic caste—the doling out of large sums of money (whether one's own or some wealthy foundation's) to the less fortunate. "Reformer" is too closely linked to politics; as vital as political reform may be, no amount of tinkering with the existing machinery of government can ever be more than one step in a program to improve the quality of life. "Humanitarian" has a nice ring to it, and it is certainly broad enough in scope, but it lacks the imperative of personal commitment; a man may be accounted a humanitarian on the basis of his sympathies alone. The only other candidates that spring to mind are "saint"—a title best conferred posthumously—and "revolutionary."

The revolutionary, like the do-gooder, sees his goal as nothing less than the eradication of injustice and the construction of a better society. But unlike the do-gooder, who tries to achieve this end without adopting unjust methods, the revolutionary proclaims that only in the distant future can ends and means be brought into harmony. In the meantime, there is a job to do; and according to the classic Marxist analysis, the conscientious do-gooder with his scruples against violent solutions actually *perpetuates* injustice, since any small success he may achieve will tend to undermine the revolutionary fervor of the oppressed —the force that alone can generate significant change. The revolutionary's slogan is brutally frank: "I must be cruel only to be kind."

By all rules of logic and common sense, this slogan and the analysis behind it ought to be unacceptable to the great majority of reform-minded, philanthropic, humanitarian, occasionally altruistic, conscientiously liberal, self-proclaimed *decent* people —like you and me, dear reader?—who are active from time to time in what are considered to be good causes. Yet implicit in our current use of the word "do-gooder" is the suspicion that the two notions of "doing good" and "getting things done" are basically irreconcilable. The same people who would recoil in horror from the thought of teaching their children that good ends justify evil means find it all too easy to concede that the profes-

sional revolutionary is somehow "more realistic" than they themselves dare to be.

It is true that most of us can still believe in personal saints,
men whose lives seem to embody an uncompromising vision of
a better world. And no one doubts that ordinary men can rise,
under the pressure of extraordinary circumstances, to a kind
of saintly behavior for a time, or that decent people can successfully band together—in a loosely structured "movement"
—to attain limited objectives. But when the saints try to organize for the long run, or the movements evolve into institutions,
that is a different matter. Such enterprises are felt to be doomed
from the start because only by compromising their ideals can
the do-gooders hope to last long enough to have any apprecia-
ble impact—and the more they compromise, the more they
come to resemble the system they are supposed to be changing.
The notion that power inevitably corrupts is an ancient one; history is full of examples of the betrayal of political and religious
reform by the successful reformers. But the argument that *any*
attempt to reform the power structure leads inevitably to co-optation is relatively new—and even more disheartening.

The collective experience of that determined band of do-
gooders known as the Quakers runs directly counter to this argument, however. From their earliest days of radical religious
dissent in seventeenth-century England, the main body of Quakers has remained dedicated to the proposition that men can and
must be both effective and compassionate, tough-minded and
tender-hearted in matters of social change. In the twentieth century this concern has found its most typical expression in the
work of organizations such as the American Friends Service
Committee. The record has hardly been one of unmitigated success. But those who are morally repelled by the alternatives—
perpetual impotence or the ruthless destruction of the status

5

ON DOING GOOD

quo—will find persuasive the fact that do-gooders can effect social change, that at certain moments in history, certain men have been able to combine the goals of "doing good" and "getting things done" on a significant scale, without succumbing to corruption, co-optation, despair, or the temptation to use violence.

PART I

ROOTS

❖ ❖ ❖

THAT OF GOD IN EVERY ONE

ONE unintentional tribute to the success of the Quaker movement in seventeenth-century England is the difficulty that historians have had in determining exactly when the movement began. It is not that the dates and events have been lost in legend or muddled in controversy; it is simply that the material does not lend itself to the usual chronological treatment. Historians must have dates (if only to avoid transposing cause and effect). Even historians of religion, who may prefer to speculate about essentially private experiences like the sudden enlightenments of Luther and Calvin, must focus whenever possible on the public manifestations of faith—the nailing of a piece of paper to a church door, or the publication of a definitive work of theology.

George Fox, who was born in a tiny village in Leicestershire in 1624, is universally acknowledged as the founder of Quakerism, but the start of his ministry was not associated with any outward drama. He never adopted any title or official position, and he established no hierarchy, promulgated no creed, and left behind no shrines or monuments on which a historian might hang a date. His major written work, the *Journal*, was published posthumously. In it, he makes clear that his first success as a preacher came when he addressed large numbers of people known as Seekers—spiritual pilgrims who had already worked out for themselves many of the beliefs that would later be considered basic to Quakerism.

Essentially, these earliest Quakers believed that the spiritual dimension was sufficient, and that a man did not have to look to an infallible Vatican or an infallible Holy Writ for justification. For convenience and mutual succor, they soon banded together in congregations known as Monthly Meetings, and in groupings of congregations known as Yearly Meetings, and they created other limited instrumentalities as need arose. (The aptly named Meeting for Sufferings was one.) But the Religious Society of Friends, as the general body of professing Quakers came to be called,° has remained without charter, leader, or headquarters. In fact, it has no corporate existence whatever apart from its individual members. (There are approximately 200,000 Quakers today, with 120,000 in the United States and 21,000 in England.)

Historians usually content themselves with describing the Quaker movement as an outgrowth of the Puritan upheavals of the 1640's and 1650's in central and northern England. When more specific dates are needed, they must be taken—on the Quakers' own terms, so to speak—from the different stages of George Fox's spiritual development. His father, Christopher, was a weaver who was known to his neighbors as "Righteous Christer" for his upright behavior. The atmosphere in the Fox household was sober and serious—Puritanical in the most basic sense. By the time he was twenty years old, George Fox had become dissatisfied with the teachings of the priests of the Established Church, who failed, as he wrote in his *Journal*, "to speak to my condition." A few years later, after searching in vain for something better among the myriad nonconforming sects of the time, he had a soul-shaking mystical experience which convinced him that the age of direct revelation had not ended with the New Testament. And in 1652, he climbed a hill in northern

---

° In a somewhat immodest reference to the words of Jesus Christ: "Henceforth I call you not servants; for the servant knoweth not what his Lord doeth; but I have called you friends" (John 15:15).

England called Pendle Hill and was vouchsafed a clear vision of a "great people" waiting to be "gathered" for the Lord.

In the years immediately following, Fox and those he had gathered set out to convince the world that there was nothing impractical about practicing what Christ had preached. They were fundamentalists concerning the spirit, not the letter, of the New Testament. They believed that it was possible to live in the world according to the moral precepts of the Sermon on the Mount, and they also believed that the Word of the Living God was still available as a guide to anyone who took care to listen. "And this I knew experimentally," George Fox wrote, to describe the "great openings" he had received from the Lord during his long pilgrimage through an England racked by Civil War.

The early Quakers styled themselves "Children of the Light" and "Publishers of the Truth," because they insisted that what they had learned was applicable to all men. In a sense they were right. Their message proved to be as disturbing to most dissenters of the day as it was to the Established Church. For their zeal in publishing the truth as they saw it, Quakers were persecuted with almost unimaginable ferocity in both Old England and New England. A volume entitled *A Collection of the Sufferings of the People Called Quakers* (published in 1753) tells of the trials of some 12,000 Friends prior to the passage of the Toleration Act of 1689. (At least 450 are estimated to have died in prison.)

When English Quakers were not being accused of treason or popery or disrespect to authority or disturbing the peace, they might be thrown in jail for failure to pay tithes, or for "recusancy"—failure to attend services of the Church of England. In colonial Massachusetts, where the fledgling Commonwealth was committed to maintaining the purity of Calvinist doctrine, the reception that awaited Quakers may be surmised from this early comment by a Puritan minister of Ipswich: "It is said that men ought to have liberty of conscience, and that it is *persecution* to debar them of it. I can rather stand amazed than reply to this. It is an astonishment that the brains of a man should be parboiled in such impious ignorance."

The latter half of the seventeenth century has been called the "heroic, or apostolic age" of the Society of Friends. While other, equally enthusiastic religious movements flowered briefly and withered away (or were cut down), the Quakers not only survived persecution but prospered—and apparently without compromising their original vision. In an effort to revive what they called "Primitive Christianity," Friends refused to bear arms, they refused to swear oaths (a serious matter in the 1600's), and they refused to acknowledge the supremacy of any church or state over the individual conscience. Yet they continued to grow in numbers and influence. Clearly, they had proved their point about the practicality of the *imitatio Christi*—or had they only proved that the more brutally the claims of reality are urged on some men, the more stubbornly they will cling to their vision of the ideal?

In the three centuries since then, the Quaker vision has undergone several major adjustments. When the heroes and apostles passed, the consolidators took over. Quietism replaced enthusiasm. The movement became a sect, the sect turned in on itself, and—in the United States especially—split apart in a series of bitter schisms, with each party accusing the other of following the letter, not the spirit, of the original Quaker faith. There were Quakers in Philadelphia and New York who insisted on maintaining the traditional "unprogrammed" meeting, where each member simply "waited upon the Lord" in silence, and stood up to speak his mind whenever he wanted to share an insight with his neighbors. And there were other Quakers in the Midwest and West who believed in changing with the times, even if this meant hiring pastors to conduct Sunday services that were enlivened with hymn-singing and responsive reading. But the underlying challenge of Quakerism—a call to remain in the world and practice what Christ preached—ensured that a certain percentage of each generation would oppose any tendency to turn the Society of Friends into just another self-perpetuating Protestant denomination, in a country where "Protestant" had become virtually a synonym for "status quo."

Quakers had been concerned with social justice from the beginning—persecution can be a great teacher in such matters —and by the time the doctrinal nit-picking of the nineteenth century was over, the inheritors of this concern had evolved a far-reaching social gospel, stressing prison reform, care of the mentally ill, racial equality, and reconciliation of differences in a nonviolent atmosphere. Since 1917, the American Friends Service Committee has been a primary instrument for testing Quaker initiatives in these areas. The guiding principles of the Service Committee are so general that Friends of every doctrinal persuasion, and sympathetic non-Friends as well, can work comfortably together. (The Committee does no proselytizing of any kind, and the great majority of the 50,000 individuals who support its work through annual donations are not members of the Religious Society of Friends.) Yet the program for reforming society that has emerged from the Committee's day-to-day operations is no less radical or ambitious than the one enunciated in the late seventeenth century by that most heroic Quaker apostle, William Penn: "A good end cannot sanctify evil means; nor must we ever do evil that good may come of it. . . . Let us then try what Love will do; for if men did once see we love them, we should soon find they would not harm us. Force may subdue, but Love gains; and he that forgives first, wins the laurel."

Traditionally, pacifism has been only one part of the Quaker program for a better world. In the beginning, it was not even the most controversial part. But as theological passions subsided, and the Friends' position on civil and religious liberties was gradually absorbed into the mainstream of Anglo-American political thought, it was only natural that outsiders would come to identify the essence of Quakerism with the Quaker Declaration of 1661, a document in which George Fox and his contemporaries explicitly renounced "all outward wars and strife and fightings with outward weapons for any end or under any pretense whatever." Many Friends still adhere to the letter of this declaration; there are Quaker Meetings in Philadelphia and New York where the tradition of conscientious objection to military service has been passed down from father to son for five and six generations. There are also Quaker Meetings in the Midwest and West where the members speak proudly of their young men who have fought in recent wars to preserve the American Way of Life. And there are still other Philadelphia Quakers who go to war and other Midwestern Quakers who go to jail rather than register for the draft. Yet with all their present diversity in religious, ethical, and political views, most active Quakers agree that there could be no such thing as Quakerism divorced from the kind of vigorous humanitarian service, conducted in an atmosphere of love and nonviolence, that the American Friends Service Committee stands for.*

* Even among Friends who do not claim to be nonviolent themselves pacifism remains a subject for serious consideration—with the rule-proving exception of some "birthright" Quakers who, like Richard Milhous Nixon, have failed to keep in touch with the wider Quaker community. Nixon's mother belonged to an old Quaker family that had been prominent in the Underground Railroad before the Civil War, and he himself was very active in the East Whittier (Calif.) Friends Meeting as a young man. He was still a Quaker when he enlisted in the U. S. Navy in 1942 (along with many other young Friends who felt that the Society's traditional peace testimony no longer "spoke to their condition"). As far as anyone knows, he has not attended a Quaker meeting in Washington since his arrival as a

Everything the Committee does is based on the belief that each human being represents an absolute value which must not be ignored, degraded, or exploited; along with this article of faith comes the acceptance of nonviolence as *a way of life,* and not just as a temporary tactic in a particular historical situation. In the world at large, anyone who seriously espouses such a philosophy can expect to be treated as a Utopian dreamer, no matter how many good deeds he may accomplish during his lifetime. Law-and-order conservatives, bewildered liberals, angry young rebels, black militants, avowed pragmatists—all find common ground in asserting that any attempt to regulate the affairs of mankind without at least the threat of a Big Stick is naïve and doomed to failure. In fact, the undeniable prevalence of this opinion is often cited as a kind of *ad hominem* proof. One might well ask why a man should be any more accurate in diagnosing his own depravity than he usually is in appraising his nobler qualities. But it is true that a widespread belief in the inevitability of violence may function as a self-fulfilling prophecy. Whenever a specific nonviolent action fails to gain its objective, the concept of nonviolence itself is discredited; when violent action fails, or wins a pyrrhic victory, the blame is laid on those who did not fight hard enough, quick enough, long enough, or cleverly enough. In such a world, the odds would appear to be hopelessly against any small band of dissenters who renounce "all outward wars and weapons." It is one thing to risk martyrdom for a good cause. But if violence is

congressman in 1947. But when he ran for the Senate in 1950, he apparently found it necessary to underscore his hard-line anti-Communism with these words: "It is not easy for me to take this position. It happens that I am a Quaker; all my training has been against displays of strength and recourse to arms. But I have learned through hard experience that, where you are confronted with a ruthless, dictatorial force that will stop at nothing to destroy you, it is necessary to defend yourself by building your own strength."

15

inevitable despite all attempts to sublimate or redirect aggressive impulses, then a nonviolent posture also entails the passive acceptance of *other* people's martyrdom. In the damning eyes of the majority, whenever the issue comes down to whether or not to bear arms against oppression, the pacifist can only be true to his scruples at the expense of his social conscience.

There are even some pacifists who concur with this argument, at least theoretically. Some of the strictest peace sects—those who base their pacifism on obedience to specific Biblical injunctions, such as "resist not evil" (Matthew 5:39)—offer the gloomiest eschatologies, with no hope whatever for the amelioration of man's suffering short of the Second Coming. Yet it is a matter of observable fact that religious pacifists in our day are far more likely to be men of the most tender social conscience, deeply concerned with the impact of their own behavior on the well-being of others. Whatever their personal reasons for rejecting violence, such men are profoundly convinced—and they feel called upon to demonstrate to the rest of mankind—that nonviolence is a practical means of ordering and improving the human condition. This extraordinarily difficult mission forms one major thread in the history of the Religious Society of Friends; and the nonviolent principles of the American Friends Service Committee can only be understood in terms of this history.

As long as the Quakers were a persecuted minority, their moral choice was a relatively simple one—martyrdom or recantation—and their loyalty to their principles could injure no one but themselves. When the period of persecution ended, and the Quakers became an accepted minority in an imperfect society, their principles (if not their courage) were put to a sterner test. The test was clearest in the New World where a group of Friends, determined to practice what they had been preaching, set out to construct a pacifist state in the middle of the American wilderness.

Their chief architect in what came to be known as the "Holy Experiment" was William Penn, who was born in London on October 14, 1644, in the second year of the armed conflict between the Puritan Parliament and the Stuart monarchy. His father, Admiral Sir William Penn, fought with distinction against the Royalist forces in the Civil War and then switched sides in time to become a favorite of Charles II after the Restoration. The younger Penn was to prove at least as nimble. He fell under the influence of religious dissenters as a young man and became an active Friend in his early twenties. Yet he somehow managed to retain his connections at the Stuart Court while becoming an important advocate of Quakerism during the days of greatest persecution. At times, anti-Quaker feeling ran so high that even Penn's courtly connections were no guarantee of safety. He spent some time in the Tower of London for publishing Quaker tracts without a license, and in 1670 he and another "Public Friend" were arrested and charged with inciting a riot for preaching to a large crowd of sympathizers in Gracechurch Street, London. The eloquent Penn argued his own case and won acquittal from the jury by appealing to the "ancient fundamental laws" of England, concerning freedom of speech and assembly. This decision so enraged the presiding magistrates that they refused to accept it, and tried to browbeat the jurors into finding the defendants guilty: "We will have a verdict, by the help of God, or you shall starve for it," the Recorder thundered. The jurors were locked up and heavily fined, but they apparently took to heart Penn's stirring words: "You are Englishmen; mind your privilege; give not away your right"—and they stood their ground. Vindication came a year later in a landmark decision of the Court of Common Pleas, which laid down the basic principle that a judge "may try to open the eyes of the jurors but not . . . lead them by the nose."

In the spring of 1680, after a decade of service to his coreligionists and to the wider cause of religious and political liberty, Penn petitioned the King for a grant of land in the New World, in payment for a £16,000 debt owing to his late father the Admiral. Charles II granted the petition—possibly as a way of ridding his kingdom of large numbers of troublesome Quakers—and on March 4, 1681, William Penn became the True and Absolute Proprietary of the province of Pennsylvania (named after his father at the King's insistence).

The Quakers were by no means strangers to the North American continent at this date. In 1656, only four years after George Fox's vision on Pendle Hill, two young women had arrived on a ship in Boston harbor with a trunkful of Quaker literature. These would-be Quaker missionaries were "stripped stark naked" by the Massachusetts authorities, searched for "tokens" of witchcraft, and imprisoned for five weeks before being shipped back to their last port of call, the West Indian island of Barbados. Their books, which were deemed to contain "corrupt, heretical, and blasphemous doctrines," were burned in the marketplace. Heresy trials, of course, were nothing new in New England; the infant colony of Rhode Island was already filling up with exiles like Anne Hutchinson and Roger Williams, who had been forced to flee from the zealous defenders of the faith in the Puritan Zion. But as self-styled "Publishers of the Truth," the early Quakers were quite the match for the Puritans when it came to zeal, although their passions were of a different sort. The Quakers kept coming to Massachusetts to share their revelation about the *universality* of the "divine Light of Christ." They believed that all men who had "the least breathing after God [could] find His power in them and with them," and they wanted to spread this good news. For devout Puritans steeped in the Calvinist doctrines of predetermination and the salvation of the elect, the Quaker gospel of a universal Inner Light was profoundly shocking. To discourage the spread of such unorthodoxy, the Boston magistrates passed a succession of laws providing increasingly harsh penalties for members of the "cursed sect" of Quakers. The laws were carried out unstintingly, but still the Quakers came. In the fall of 1657, two Friends were arrested in the town of Salem for attempting to speak to the congregation after the regular Sunday morning service. They were taken to Boston, beaten, and thrown into an unheated cell where they were held for three days without food and water. Their total imprisonment lasted nine weeks; during this time they were whipped twice a week with a "three-cord knotted whip" until each man had received more than 350 lashes. Meanwhile, a new law had been passed, specifying a fine of £100 for anyone responsible for bringing a Quaker into the colony, and forty shillings *per hour* for the crime of concealing or entertaining a Quaker. (As these provisions indicate, the Puritan Fathers were aware that there were people in Massachusetts who did not appreciate the efforts being made to save their souls from contamination.) In addition, the new law stated that any Quaker rash enough to return to the Colony after being whipped and imprisoned was to have one ear cut off for each of the next two transgressions, and his tongue bored through with a hot iron for the third. The first Quakers to test this new law, in the summer of 1658, were the same two men who had been seized in Salem the preceding fall. After a period of recuperation in the West Indies and Rhode Island, they felt "moved" to return to Massachusetts, where they were again arrested. This time they were interrogated by Governor John Endicott himself, perhaps the most zealous of all the Puritan Fathers. "I was much tempted to say I came to town to take shipping," one of the Quakers wrote later, "but I could not deny Him who moved me to come hither, nor His service, to avoid sufferings."

The Quakers lost an ear apiece, and the leaders of the Colony realized that nothing short of the ultimate penalty could quench such "firebrands." Accordingly, the General Court approved a statute making it a capital offense for a banished Quaker to return to Massachusetts.

The response of the Quakers was predictable; they felt commanded by God to go "into the Lion's den to look their Bloody laws in the Face." The Puritan Fathers were as good as their word. Despite the growing opposition of a segment of the citizenry, four Quaker missionaries—three men and a woman—were hanged on Boston Common between October 27, 1659, and March 14, 1661. All refused to recant when given the opportunity. After 1661 there were no more executions (partly because public reaction had been so negative) but a new law was substituted—the infamous Cart and Whip Act—which stated that "any person manifesting himself to be a Quaker" was to be stripped to the waist, tied to a cart's tail, and whipped from one town to the next, to the farthest border of the Colony.

The worst forms of persecution came to an end four years later, with the death of Governor Endicott and the arrival of an order from the Royal Commissioners in London, forbidding any further interference with loyal subjects of the Crown who happened to be Quakers. (This order was the result of some persistent lobbying by influential Friends in the home country.) For the next decade, the authorities in Massachusetts stayed their hand, but with obvious reluctance. Then, in 1675, when one of the bloodiest of the Indian wars that had plagued the Bay Colony almost from its inception broke out, a Day of Humiliation was proclaimed by the Puritan divines. In this proclamation, the war was characterized as God's judgment on the backsliding Christians of New England for such sins as neglecting the education of the young, behaving rudely during worship, wearing long hair—and failing to suppress the Quaker heresy. To back up the proclamation, a new law was passed, providing a five-pound fine and imprisonment on bread and water for anyone found guilty of attending a Quaker meeting.

The nearby colony of Rhode Island, which was now governed by Quakers, had good reason to doubt the Puritans' explanation for the new outbreak of Indian hostilities. Besides being a haven of religious tolerance in a maelstrom of sectarian fanaticism—the Puritans referred to it as the "island of error"—Rhode Island was also an anomaly in its relations with the Indians. Roger Williams had laid down a policy of fair payment to the natives for any land settled on; and the Quaker governors had not only continued this policy, but had tried to guarantee the Indians equal rights under provincial law: an Indian accused of murder was entitled to trial by a jury that was half Indian, and the testimony of an Indian was to be given the same credence in court as that of an Englishman. This was in marked contrast to the policies of the other New England colonies; in general, the Puritan Fathers believed that the Indians were the children of Satan, and acted accordingly. In 1637, for instance, when the Pequot tribe offered resistance to the tide of European settlement in southern Connecticut, a war party from the Massachusetts Bay Colony set fire to the principal Pequot village, immolating most of the inhabitants—men, women and children—in their homes. Those trying to escape were shot, or captured and sold into slavery. Cotton Mather recorded the event in his journal with obvious satisfaction: "On this day we have sent six hundred heathen souls to hell."

The Indian uprising of 1675 in New England is usually referred to as "King Philip's War," because it was led by an Indian chief known to the settlers by that name. King Philip was the son of Massasoit, the grand sachem of the Wampanoag tribe, who had greeted the first English Pilgrims so hospitably in 1620. To judge by the accounts of the Europeans themselves, hospitality toward strangers seems to have been a characteristic of all the "savages" of the New World, from the coast of Maine to the southern tip of Peru. But in New England, as in most other places, the era of good feelings between the races did not last long. Within a few years, the Indians were complaining about ill-treatment by the English, especially the Puritans of Massachusetts Bay. After the death of Massasoit, tensions increased, and Philip devoted himself to forging an alliance of New England tribes to drive the settlers out. In the spring of 1675, when it became apparent that the Indians were ready to resort to warfare, a party of five Rhode Island Quakers went unarmed to King Philip's headquarters on Narragansett Bay, to see if there might be still some peaceful way to resolve the conflict. According to a narrative of the conference in the hand of John Easton, deputy-governor of Rhode Island, Philip's grievances were both political and personal: he demanded satisfaction for the alleged poisoning of his uncle by a white man; he decried the eagerness of some Englishmen "to sell the Indians liquor [so] that most Indians spent all in drunkenness and then raved up on the sober Indians"; and he spoke eloquently about the indignities that his people had suffered before the white man's law in New England: "If twenty of their honest Indians testified that an Englishman had done them wrong [the third-person narrative continues], it was nothing, but if one of their worst Indians testified against any Indian, [even] their King, when it pleased the English, it was sufficient."

The Rhode Island Quakers told Philip that their only desire "was that the quarrel might be rightly decided in the best way, not as dogs decide their quarrels." When the Indians agreed that "fighting was the worst way" to settle a dispute, the Quakers suggested arbitration by two outside parties, the British Governor of New York and an Indian chief of Philip's own choosing. The Indians said that they had never heard of such a procedure, but they seemed interested, and John Easton comments, "We were persuaded that if this way had been tendered they would have accepted." But the Quakers could not convince the Indians that the other New England colonies would go along with arbitration. (In fact, the Puritan Fathers were incensed at the Quakers for daring to suggest that there might be any truth in the grievances of the heathen.)

The war began a few days later and lasted until the summer of 1676. The toll was fearful—fifty-two of the ninety white settlements in New England were attacked, and twelve were destroyed; most of the Indian villages in King Philip's alliance were wiped out. The surviving Indian captives, including Philip's widow and son, were sold into slavery; the King's body was dismembered and his head stuck on a pole for public viewing.

For their attempt to avert such mutual butchery and for their failure to assume a full military posture once the hostilities had begun, the Rhode Island Quakers were accused of complicity in the death of white men. This same charge would be heard against the Quakers of Pennsylvania, together with the Quaker reply that there would have been no war if all the settlers had treated the Indians fairly.

Despite the horrors of King Philip's War, and the angry polemics that followed, the Quakers' foothold in North America continued to expand. By the time William Penn became proprietor of Pennsylvania, members of the Society of Friends already formed an important element in the population of several English colonies, and they had reason to believe that the seeds of their "Primitive Christianity" would find particularly fertile soil in the New World. They had survived the fiery furnace of Massachusetts; they had won so many converts in Rhode Island that they now dominated that colony's politics (although they were never a majority). Their influence was also dominant in New Jersey, which had passed into the control of a group of Quaker proprietors (including Penn himself) in the previous decade; and Quaker settlers were flocking to North Carolina, where liberty of conscience was guaranteed by the Fundamental Law

23

ON DOING GOOD

drafted by John Locke. In this heady atmosphere of fresh starts
and released energies, all things seemed possible, and Penn's
plans for his new colony were nothing if not grandiose: "The nations want a precedent—and because I have been somewhat exercised about the nature and end of government among men, it
is reasonable to expect that I should endeavour to establish a
just and righteous one in this province that others may take example by it. . . . There may be room there [that is, in Ameri-
ca], though not here [that is, in England] for such a holy experiment."

Among his other "experimental" notions, Penn really seemed
to believe that the commonwealth of free men he was founding
was for free *red* men as well as white men. He went so far as to
study what was known of the habits of the indigenous population, and before setting foot on the soil of Pennsylvania he sent
a letter to the Indians announcing his intentions. The agent who
carried this letter was instructed to "be grave [for] they loved
not to be smiled on." The letter itself has been described by
Francis Jennings, a non-Quaker historian whose research has
recently thrown new light on the fate of Quaker policies in
colonial Pennsylvania, as "a unique document in the literature of
Indian-European relations."

> My friends [the letter begins]—there is one great God and
> power that hath made the world and all things therein, to
> whom you and I, and all people owe their being and well-
> being, and to whom you and I must one day give an account for
> all that we do in the world. . . . Now this great God hath
> been pleased to make me concerned in your parts of the world,
> and the king of the country where I live hath given unto me a
> great province, but I desire to enjoy it with your love and con-
> sent, that we may always live together as neighbours and
> friends, else what would the great God say to us, who hath
> made us not to devour and destroy one another, but live so-

berly and kindly together in the world? . . . I am very sensible of the unkindness and injustice that hath been too much exercised towards you by the people of these parts of the world, who sought . . . to make great advantages by you . . . which I hear hath been matter of trouble to you, and caused great grudgings and animosities, sometimes to the shedding of blood, which hath made the great God angry; but I am not such a man, as is well known in my own country . . . and the people I send are of the same mind, and shall in all things behave themselves accordingly; and if in any thing any shall offend you or your people, you shall have full and speedy satisfaction for the same, by an equal number of just men on both sides, that by no means you may have just occasion of being offended against them. I shall shortly come to you myself, at what time we may more largely and freely confer and discourse of these matters. . . . [The letter is signed] I am your loving friend, William Penn.

Penn's attitude toward the Indians was, in a sense, predetermined by the Quakers' conviction that *all* men are enlightened by God's Truth, no matter who they are, where they live, or what idols they pay homage to. The Quakers apparently started out with vague hopes of making Friends, as well as friends, of the Indians; some early missionaries even discerned a similarity between the Indians' Great Spirit and the Inner Light. But actual proselytizing proved difficult for a sect that had no creed, no sacraments, and no liturgy. The Quaker missionary had a specific message only for the devout Christian who was dissatisfied with the present state of his church. To such a seeker the Quaker could say: "The answer lies in giving up all creeds, sacraments, and liturgies; learn instead to wait upon the Lord." But to the heathen, the Quaker could offer only the kind of testimony described by George Fox in one of his famous admonitory epistles: "Be patterns, be examples in all countries, places, islands, nations, wherever you come, that your carriage and life may preach among all sorts of people, and to them; then you will come to walk cheerfully over the world, answering that of God in every one." When Fox himself visited the American colonies in 1672–73, he walked (and rode) cheerfully from Maryland to Rhode Island and back south again; his accounts of meetings with the natives usually end with the phrase, "And they appeared very loving to us." Other traveling Friends reported similar experiences; in the early Quaker journals, the Indians often figure as benign presences, offering sanctuary from the cruelty and violence of white persecutors. In a typical instance, two Quakers who were forced to flee from Puritan wrath were assured by their Indian protectors, "The Quakers are honest men, and do no harm, and this is no Englishman's sea or land, and the Quakers shall come here and welcome." One of the Quakers later recorded his reaction: "I do confess, through the goodness of the Lord we found these Indians more sober and Christian-like toward us than the Christians so-called."

The good ship *Welcome* brought William Penn to his province for the first time in the fall of 1682. One of his first official acts was to call together a representative assembly—from the handful of European settlers who were already living along the Delaware River—and preside over the enactment of fundamental legislation, including many of the guarantees of personal and political liberty that the Quakers had been agitating for on both sides of the Atlantic for the past quarter-century.

While the Pennsylvania settlers were experimenting with their new form of representative government (differences of opinion about the constitution sprang up almost immediately), the proprietor was experimenting with a new approach to Indian diplomacy. His approach might be called "Utopian" in the sense that he expected the natives to live peaceably side by side with the settlers. But it was solidly grounded on the experiences of many traveling Friends, and on an understanding of the successes and failures of the other American colonies. In addition, Penn took the time to learn the language of the Leni-Lenape tribe—the Indians who inhabited the Delaware Valley.

Penn at this time was a vigorous man of thirty-eight, and legend has it that he participated in the Indians' feast of roasted acorns, excelled in their jumping contests and other athletic competitions, and in general won their confidence by his grave demeanor, expressions of brotherly love, and assurances of fair treatment in all matters concerning land and trade. Again according to legend, a Great Treaty of Friendship was signed under a spreading elm at the Lenape village of Shackamaxon (now the Kensington section of Philadelphia). This treaty was later apostrophized by Voltaire as the only agreement between Europeans and Indians "never sworn to and never broken," and Benjamin West painted a famous but wildly anachronistic canvas of the event. Because no copy of the agreement has survived, some historians doubt that a single "Great Treaty" was signed, but all agree that Penn and the Lenape Indians came to an understanding about their peaceful coexistence in the Delaware Valley. Penn himself reported meeting with the Indians, and noted that "Great promises passed between us of Kindness and good Neighbourhood, and that the Indians and English must live in love as long as the Sun give light." A hundred years later the old men of the Lenape tribe recalled the event to a missionary in almost exactly the same words.

This mutual understanding was the principal bulwark against attack and intimidation erected by the Quaker colony of Pennsylvania, which for the next seventy-five years enjoyed virtual immunity from the Indian wars that periodically ravaged the other European settlements in North America. Yet when the "Long Peace" in Pennsylvania came to an end with the French and Indian War of 1756, the corpses were piled—figuratively, and sometimes literally—on the doorsteps of the Quaker authorities. Once again, as in King Philip's War, Quakers were blamed for not arming the populace quickly enough or well enough. Once again, Quakers replied that there would have been no war if the Indians had received fair treatment from all the colonists, in the tradition of Roger Williams and William Penn.

In retrospect, several facts are clear. According to "The History of Violence in America," a report submitted in 1969 to the National Commission on the Causes and Prevention of Violence:

> Unquestionably the longest and most remorseless war in American history was the one between whites and Indians that began in Tidewater, Virginia, in 1607 and continued with only temporary truces for nearly 300 years down to the final massacre at Wounded Knee, South Dakota in 1890.

Furthermore, all the history books agree that the longest and steadiest truce in that war was the one which, for seventy-five years, kept Pennsylvania the most secure as well as the most prosperous province on a continent seething with racial, religious, commercial and military conflict. And yet most historians —except for the avowed Quaker apologists—have focused their attention *not* on the existence of the Long Peace (or on the implications to be drawn from it), but on the hostilities that brought it to an end; such writers either treat the pacifism of the Quaker leaders as circumstantial to the success of William Penn's commonwealth, or they argue that Pennsylvania enjoyed peace and prosperity *despite* a pacifist government—whose naïve Indian policies eventually brought about its own downfall, along with the massacre of untold numbers of innocents in the backwoods of the province.

Sophisticated historians never tire of asserting, for the benefit of unsophisticated laymen, that the study of the past cannot really "prove" anything. Even the work of the most conscientiously objective scholar reflects the intellectual milieu in which it is written, and must be considered open to revision as changing times offer fresh perspectives. But the attempt to keep history free, at the very least, of the prejudices and distortions of past historians is enormously important—since both scholars and laymen persist in applying lessons from history to present actions. Can anyone doubt that black Americans have suffered because our history books held up to us for so long such a one-sided picture of "reality"? If another kind of distortion has led historians to misread the lessons of the Holy Experiment, we may all be suffering the consequences.

Admittedly, the historical drama that unfolded in colonial Pennsylvania was no simple morality play. Not all Pennsylvania leaders were Quakers, and not all Pennsylvania Quakers were strict pacifists, and there were many other actors on the stage, including the forces of the rival British and French empires, commercial entrepreneurs and political adventurers from at least three neighboring colonies, an uncontrollable influx of non-Quaker settlers with ideas of their own, and, at one time or another, nearly all the Indian tribes in the northeastern quarter of the continent. In addition, the official archives are even less trustworthy than usual, because during most of the colonial period they were in the exclusive keeping of people who had scores to settle and schemes of their own to hide. And aside from all these difficulties, a historian must contend with the factor of Indian illiteracy—which means that motives of the tribes involved are known only through the testimony of white interpreters and observers, whose objectivity is often suspect. Under such circumstances, sorting out the evidence and drawing conclusions is especially difficult. But given the undeniable existence of the Long Peace in a state founded by pacifists, the burden of argument would seem to lie with those who deny a cause-and-effect relationship. Pragmatists will note, at the very least, that pacifism did *not* bring instant ruin to Pennsylvania. (If nonviolence were really so contrary to human nature, then a state built on pacifist principles—even under the most ideal conditions—could not be expected to last seventy-five days, much less seventy-five years.)

The question remains, What *did* go wrong in the end? Was the collapse of the Holy Experiment in Pennsylvania inevitable? Did it result from external factors beyond the control of the Quakers and their provincial allies? Or was there some flaw in the social fabric that undermined the ambitious political and diplomatic structure that William Penn had erected? In the world of today, threatened as we are with extinction in one more "practical" war, it may not be impractical to go over the lessons of the Holy Experiment once again, from the pacifist point of view—first, to see how a pacifist policy *might* have been responsible for keeping the peace for so long; and second, to suggest an explanation, consistent with the first hypothesis, for the ultimate return to the law of musket and tomahawk along the Pennsylvania frontier.

To get a better understanding of what actually happened in Pennsylvania, it is important at the start to clear up some popular misconceptions. The Indians who greeted the first white settlers along the Middle Atlantic seaboard were not the footloose, individualistic children of the primeval forest so often portrayed in romance and legend. All the available evidence indicates that they were not nomads, they were not loners, and they were not even primarily hunters and trappers. Instead they lived in tightly knit, complex social units based in permanent, sometimes rather elaborate villages, and their diet consisted largely of corn, squash, and beans which they cultivated in garden plots they had cleared themselves near their homes. To supplement these agricultural staples, entire villages might decamp on seasonal

hunting and fishing expeditions, but the villagers always returned to their homes and fields, even when the round-trip jour-
neys involved distances of hundreds of miles. There were some
large-scale migrations in the period just prior to the arrival of
the white man, but those were due mainly to the exhaustion of
local food supplies or to the fortunes of war. In general, the Indians of the northeastern woodlands had a clear idea of which
tribe belonged on which piece of land at any given moment;
hospitality to strangers was the general custom, but challenges
to territorial interests met with a violent response. History and
legend, however, agree on one important point: most tribes were
quite willing to sign over their interest in the land to the settlers
—if the price was right.

Even in the earliest days, when the European settlements
were no more than tiny beachheads dependent for their very existence on Indian aid and goodwill, the red man recognized the
obvious superiority of the white man's tools and weapons. In a
sense, the real conquest of North America began and ended the
moment the first Indian decided that the hardware of the new-
comers was worth bartering for. Unfortunately for the red man,
the technological gap between the two cultures was so great
that there would always be, in Francis Jennings' words, "a fundamental inequality" in their relations:

> After the Europeans had been taught how to make and use ca-
> noes, moccasins, buckskin clothing and impromptu shelters, they
> could dispense with further Indian guidance. But Indians
> learned only how to use European tools and weapons; they did
> not also learn how to make them. Becoming addicted to the su-
> perior European products, the Indians soon lost their own neo-
> lithic skills through disuse, and thus became perpetually de-
> pendent on European sources of supply. In the trade which
> thus came to dominate their economy, the Indians were limited
> to supplying the commodities desired by the whites. Apart from

occasional personal service, the Indians' only commodities of value were [furs] and lands.

One transaction recorded in the early days of the colony of West Jersey suggests the impact that the white man's arrival must have had on the indigenous culture. In exchange for the right to settle on some land near the present site of Burlington, the Quaker colonists paid over the following:

> 30 matchcoats, 20 guns, 30 kettles, and one great one, 30 pair hose, 20 fathom of duffields, 30 petticoats, 30 narrow hoes, 30 bars of lead, 15 small barrels of powder, 70 knives, 30 Indian axes, 70 combs, 60 pair tobacco tongs, 60 scissors, 69 tinshaw looking-glasses, 120 awl-blades, 120 fish-hooks, 2 grasps of red paint, 120 needles, 60 tobacco boxes, 120 pipes, 200 bells, 100 Jews' harps, 6 anchors rum.

The Indians were not slow to realize the implications of their technological "inequality." Even when they went on the warpath to avenge real or imagined grievances, they had to be careful not to cut themselves off entirely from future supplies. According to a contemporary account, the chief of a neighboring tribe dissuaded the Leni-Lenape from attacking pre-Quaker settlements in the Delaware Valley, by using the argument that "here live Christians and there live Christians, [and] as they were surrounded by Christians, if they went to war, where would they get powder and ball?"

As for the Christians themselves, most of them were aware from the beginning of the peculiar terms of their relationship with the Indians. In 1622, a settler in Virginia argued with his neighbors that "it is not fitting utterly to make an extirpation of the Savages *yet*, [because] they have ever kept down the woods and slain the wolves, bears and other beasts," which might have otherwise inconvenienced the English farmers. However, once the initial settlement was secured, then it was the "savages" who became an inconvenience; and it was doubly "fitting" to clear off the Indians by military action, since there could be no better title to land than the universally recognized right of conquest. In 1644, the governor of the province of New Sweden, one of several short-lived jurisdictions on Delaware Bay that preceded the establishment of Pennsylvania, asked his superiors to send over a troop of soldiers to "break the necks" of the Lenape, because (the governor wrote) "When we have not only bought this river but also won it with the sword, then no one, whether he be Hollander or Englishman, could pretend in any manner to this place either now or in coming times." Similar policies were pursued by the Dutch in New York and the Puritans in New England, both of whom offered bounties for Indian scalps in an effort to "clear the land."

As a loyal courtier and a man of his time, William Penn never doubted that the charter given him by his Christian sovereign made him the lord of a vast tract of real estate bounded on the north by New York, on the south by Maryland, on the east by New Jersey, and on the west by the mapmaker's imagination. But as a good Quaker, Penn also believed that the aborigines had a "natural right" to the land they lived on, and before disposing of any part of his assigned domain, he proposed to extinguish the Indian claims by purchasing an unexceptionable title, acre by acre, directly from the local inhabitants. The prices that he paid were more than generous. Between 1682 and 1685, he spent at least £1,200 for a small triangle of land in the southeast corner of the province, around the site of his new capital, Philadelphia. (Such liberality cannot be dismissed as a mere gesture of goodwill by a sanctimonious Croesus, because the Penn family finances were in extremely shaky condition during most of this period.)

When Penn learned that the Indians with whom he had dealt so fairly (one was a chief named Tamanend, or Taminiy, or

33

more popularly Tammany) were coming back to demand further payments for the same piece of land, he was at first furious. He had returned to England in 1684 to defend his interests in a boundary dispute with Lord Baltimore, but he instructed his agent in Pennsylvania to see that the natives were punished by the magistrates for not keeping their part of the bargain: "If they see that you use them severely when roguish and kindly when just, they will demean themselves accordingly." Like most of the early Quakers, Penn was by no means a passive pacifist; the Society of Friends has always supported the reasonable use of physical constraints to enforce the ordinances of a legally constituted state. But rather than press the issue—Tammany had threatened to burn down the Englishmen's houses unless his demands were met—Penn eventually paid for the same land a *second* time, and then once again.

On the surface, this incident would appear to be a perfect example of the inapplicability of Quaker ideals to the operations of government: the well-meaning pacifist bends over backwards to be decent to the wily savage, and gets bullied in return. Indeed, one school of American historians views the entire Holy Experiment in this light. In his influential study, *The Americans: The Colonial Experience* (1957), Daniel J. Boorstin wrote: "The political success, even the very survival of an American colony, often depended on a realistic estimate of the Indian. But the Quakers' view of the Indian was of a piece with their attitude toward war: it was unrealistic, inflexible, and based on false premises about human nature."

Yet there is good reason to believe, from recent findings of anthropologists and the new breed of "ethnohistorians," that the idea of owning absolute title to a piece of land—and therefore the possibility of selling such title—was as unimaginable to the Lenape Indian as the idea of owning or selling a piece of the Atlantic Ocean would be to us. What the Indians apparently thought they were doing when they accepted payment from Penn's agents, was to sign over, for a limited time, "the rights of use for residence and subsistence" on the territory traditionally under their control. Curiously, this concept was not really so alien from certain medieval practices that were still current in seventeenth-century England. For example, as the True and Absolute Proprietary of Pennsylvania, William Penn was careful to include in every land sale to European settlers the provision for an annual "quitrent" of one shilling per hundred acres. Under Old World feudal law, a quitrent was a small cash payment due to the lord of manor from a freeholder in lieu of personal services. One shilling per hundred acres per year sounds small enough; but for an entire province, the shillings added up. Penn himself estimated the sum due to him for the year 1686, when the settlement of Pennsylvania had barely begun, at about £500. And the quitrents were to be paid by the settlers and their heirs to the proprietor and his heirs *in perpetuity*. As Jennings notes, it makes an interesting comparison: "Penn and his heirs looked forward to a perpetual income from quitrents even as the Lenape looked forward to perpetually renewed presents."

In European terms, then, Chief Tammany may have been demanding the next installment of rent—or, possibly, increasing it, on the landlordly assumption that the settlers were using the land more intensely than he had anticipated. (Indian customs permitted either party to a "contract" to reopen negotiations at any time if he felt that more compensation was called for.) Whatever his motives, it seems likely that Tammany was behaving according to the standards of conduct dictated by his own culture, however strange those standards might have seemed to outsiders. When William Penn gave in to Tammany's demands rather than resort to violence, he was acting—whether he knew it or not—on a more "realistic" estimate of the Lenape in particular and of human nature in general than those settlers who saw

35

the Indians as Children of Satan or Children of Nature, given to capricious quirks of savagery, and governable only by the rod.

Obviously, though, there remained a dangerous failure of communication that had to be overcome before the men of the two cultures could live "soberly and kindly" together. The compromise worked out—without violence on either side—seems to have been based on an early model of the Indian reservation: For an agreed-upon fee, Lenape villages explicitly surrendered all claims of local "sovereignty" to William Penn, who then guaranteed that they and their heirs would forever enjoy residential and hunting rights, and equal protection under provincial laws. This system was apparently in operation by the turn of the century; after 1700 the records show no more cases of double or triple compensation for the same land. Unfortunately, the creation of Indian reservations also created doubts about the legal rights of the original inhabitants—doubts which were later exploited by men who did not share the Founder's vision of a pluralistic society.

It was a sad fact of the American frontier that only a man of the strongest moral fiber could be expected to resist the temptation to cheat Indians. Not only were the rewards enormous (there was a whole continent to buy and sell), but, at least in the beginning, no one was easier to cheat. Confronted with European tools and weapons, the Indians had to trade to live; they usually had to deal in a tightly controlled market; and since they had no writing, all documents recording transactions between the races were under the control of white men.

Before the Europeans arrived, Indian "records" had been stored in the heads of tribal elders, who witnessed all important events, such as treaties, and passed their recollections along to their successors, together with ceremonial belts of wampum which depicted the events in rough hieroglyphics and served as

36

mnemonic aids. Orderly relations between neighboring tribes were difficult enough to maintain—with the inevitable territorial disputes, personal vendettas, and the young braves' pursuit of martial glory for its own sake—but there could have been no order at all in Indian society if the memories of the treaty-makers and record-keepers had not been generally trustworthy. Later, when disputes arose between Indians and white men, the Indians discovered that it was their remembered word against the white men's written word. Sometimes, the white men's documents contained words that the tribal elders did not remember. Sometimes, a crucial piece of paper, which the elders remembered, had disappeared from the white men's files. Not surprisingly, the Indians' reputation for truth-telling did not do them much good in such arguments. But even those white men who made a living out of cheating red men have left testimonials (in private correspondence) to the reliability of the Indians' solemnly given word—at least in the days before the savages were thoroughly "civilized" by exposure to European politics, business practices, and liquor.

If any group of settlers could have been expected to deal honorably with the Indians on their own terms, it was the Quakers. In refusing to swear oaths—even an oath of allegiance to their king—the Quakers had committed themselves to that unequivocal standard of honesty extolled in the Sermon on the Mount. The smallest falsehood, even if unintended, was considered a breach of faith, and the Quakers cultivated an art of understatement that was sometimes carried to extremes.° Yet unlike the illiterate Indian, for whom truth-telling was a habit *reinforced* by

---

° In the classic anecdote about the scrupulously honest Quaker, two pillars of the Society are passing a field in which some recently shorn sheep are grazing; one says, "Friend, I see that these sheep have been shorn," to which the other replies, "Well, at least they have been shorn on the side facing the road."

social necessity, the Quakers' devotion to plain speech was a conscientious effort to practice a higher morality *in spite of* the world's temptations; and as such it was only as strong as each individual's conscience.

The remarkable material prosperity attained by the Pennsylvania colony within a few years of its settlement has been carefully documented by Frederick Tolles, a Quaker historian at Swarthmore College. In his book *Meeting House and Counting House* (1948) Tolles writes that Philadelphia rose rapidly "to unchallenged commercial superiority in colonial America—a position surpassed in the whole British Empire only by London and Bristol." With typically Quakerish understatement he adds that the Quakers themselves played "no inconsiderable part" in this success story. In 1769, at a time when members of the Society of Friends probably constituted no more than one-seventh of the city's population, Quakers made up more than half of those Philadelphians paying taxes in excess of £100. And of the seventeen wealthiest men in the city that year, "eight were Quakers in good standing, four were men who had been reared in the faith," and one had inherited the basis of his fortune from a Quaker grandfather.*

More important than the mere fact of this great wealth, however, is the story of how it was made. Compared to the violent clash of cultures elsewhere on the continent, there is not much overt drama in the test of conscience that Quaker entrepreneurs faced whenever opportunities to exploit the local Indians arose. But the working out of the Quaker economic ethic in Pennsylvania—as seen most vividly in the career of William Penn's ubiquitous provincial agent, James Logan—had a profound effect on the chain of events that led from the peaceful powwow at Shackamaxon to the bloody collision between white

* Another old joke about the Quakers in America makes the point more succinctly: "They came here to do good, and did very well indeed."

settlers and red warriors in 1756. And these events, in turn, have had an incalculable impact on latterday attitudes toward non-violence as a credible public posture.

According to Tolles, the Quakers had first acquired a reputation as "shrewd and successful" business entrepreneurs in the home country, where they prospered in the teeth of legal and extralegal harassment. In Pennsylvania, freed from all restraints (except a religious scruple against trading in slaves), Quaker merchants soon outstripped even their New England competitors in the complicated triangular trade; shipping grain and other agricultural commodities from Philadelphia to the West Indies; sugar, molasses, rum and wine from the West Indies to England; and articles like hardware and drygoods (which the colonists were forbidden by British Imperial policy to make for themselves) from England back to Philadelphia.

As profitable as this triangular trade could be, it was also precarious; a paper fortune made on one leg of a voyage might be lost on the next landfall (if prices had plummeted unexpectedly in a distant market), and the longer at sea, the greater the danger of a ship's sinking and dragging an otherwise flourishing business down with it. Direct trade with England was obviously preferable, but of all the trade goods available in Pennsylvania, only two were in great demand in England itself—furs and land. The taste for furs, in the form of beaver hats and the like, had become an insatiable passion among the well-to-do by the end of the seventeenth century; and the vast tracts of "undeveloped" land were a magnet not only to the hard-pressed peasantry and religious nonconformists of western Europe, but also to the English Whig oligarchs, whose love of political liberty was matched only by their devotion to real property.

Two years before the founding of Pennsylvania, no less an authority than William Penn had listed the enjoyment of property among the three fundamental rights of Englishmen, along with

39

ON DOING GOOD

representative government and trial by jury. In fact, so closely
were these concepts intertwined in the political philosophy of
the day, that no one—Quaker or non-Quaker—saw any incom-
patibility between Penn's grandiose philanthropic plans and his
desire to repair his shaky finances through a personal stake in
the riches of his province. Pennsylvania was to be a Holy Experiment in religious and political liberty, but it was also a
piece of real estate that had been given to him by the king; and
Penn had unabashedly defined property in one of his pamphlets
as "an Ownership and undisturbed possession: That which
[men] have, is rightly theirs, and no Body's else."

As it turned out, Penn's colonial proprietorship was anything
but undisturbed. The steward of his patrimonial estates in Ireland was revealed to be a master embezzler, whose machinations were so successful that Penn was eventually forced into
bankruptcy, and actually had to spend some time in debtors'
prison before other English Friends could bail him out. As a result of his financial and personal problems at home, he was able
to spend only four years in Pennsylvania—1682–84 and
1699–1701. This meant that his interests in the province had to
be placed in the hands of a trusted agent, and Penn's choice of
subordinates was not always the happiest. As his agent in Pennsylvania, Penn chose a young man named James Logan, who
had come over from England with him on his second voyage.

Logan's father, a Scottish schoolteacher, had been a minister
of the Established Church until his conversion to Quakerism in
1671, three years before the birth of his second son. Like many
other birthright Quakers, James Logan was never a "strict professor" of his parents' faith. Among other things, he believed
that defensive war was morally justified, which put him at odds
with the thoroughgoing pacifists among his coreligionists. (According to legend, the ship that brought Penn and Logan to
Pennsylvania in 1699 was attacked at sea by pirates; Logan

40

stayed on deck to help fight off the attackers, while Penn went below to pray.) But Penn did not let doctrinal differences interfere with his appreciation of Logan's quick mind and obvious administrative ability. These traits became abundantly manifest in the years following Penn's return to England, when Logan parlayed his position as guardian of the Proprietary interests into enormous political power and a lucrative business in both furs and land. The key to success in these two ventures lay in access to the local Indian population, and it was no coincidence that Logan, as Penn's agent, was *solely* responsible for the province's Indian relations.

In the early years, there was no apparent conflict between the goals of the Founder's pacifist diplomacy and the economics of the "Indian trade." As we have seen, the last thing the average European settler wanted, once his homestead had been cleared and secured, was Indian neighbors. But men of broader vision, like Logan, realized that a body of friendly, economically dependent Indians within trading distance of white settlements could serve both as a source of income and as a bulwark against possible attack by unfriendly tribes. During the first decade of the eighteenth century the legacy of Penn's humanitarian initiatives and Logan's mercantile policies actually complemented each other; together they attracted to Pennsylvania not only white settlers fleeing from persecution in the Old (or New) World, but also Indians who had been displaced in tribal wars or who were dissatisfied with the sharp practices that prevailed at the older trading centers in the neighboring colonies.

One of the bands of hunting, trapping, and trading Indians that found a temporary refuge in William Penn's province was the Shawnee, who had been dislodged from their homeland in the west sometime earlier. Some latterday observers have sought to "explain away" the achievement of Pennsylvania's Long Peace by claiming that Penn and the Quakers were just lucky in their choice of local Indians—that the Leni-Lenape were pacific and docile by nature. One trouble with this explanation is that it fails to account for the difficulty that other European settlers had with the Lenape in the Delaware Valley before the Quakers arrived; it also fails to account for the ferocity of these same Lenape warriors in the French and Indian War. But above all, it fails to account for the Shawnee. Two ethnohistorians ° who have studied this tribe extensively characterize them in these words:

> Of all our eastern peoples, the Shawnee held best to certain ideal Indian patterns of behavior: fearlessness; contempt for property and comfort; arrogance toward Whites; disregard for authority; reserve; unbridled, forthright expression of aggression, and other emotions. They were the first of the eastern North American tribes to be torn loose from the agricultural economy, sedentary and secure town life, and extreme ethnocentrism of the primitive village community. Tribes which had preceded them through the fire in the coastal regions had not survived, or had survived as remnants partly absorbed into European culture, as in New England. Tribes who would later pass through similar crises, Delaware, Sioux, Crow, Kickapoo, and others, came to acquire similar patterns of nomadism, flight, and militarism, but never with the arrogance and devil-may-care spirit of the Shawnee. We are in recent years coming to see that the violent, precarious, flamboyant lives of these peoples on the frontiers were new phenomena, the behavior of those who had survived the destruction of a peasant-village life and of all moorings of their old ways, in a world strangely and exceedingly modified by Europe.

These are the people with whom Penn had to deal in the spring of 1701 on his last visit to America. Apparently, they re-

° John Witthoft and William A. Hunter, *Ethnohistory*, II (1955). As cited in Jennings.

sponded favorably to his overtures of friendship and his offer of
mutually satisfactory trade relations. A detailed treaty was
drawn up and signed; the Shawnees preserved their copy of it
proudly for more than fifty years, long after William Penn's
death and the Indians' removal from Pennsylvania by forces beyond even their capacity to resist.

For a time, though, peace was maintained, the so-called Indian
trade flourished, the settlers prospered and multiplied—and
James Logan's personal wealth and power increased. We have
Logan's own testimony that a Philadelphia fur merchant of
those days could double his assets in sterling every two or three
years. The smart merchant profited in both directions on every
transaction; Logan's records show that he made even higher
profits on the goods that he imported from England to sell to
the Indians than he did on the pelts that he bought from the Indians to ship back to London. His markup on manufactured
goods—such as the coarse English woolens that the Indians
prized so highly—was 150 percent. Still, there were other successful merchants pursuing their "Callings" in the City of Brotherly Love, charging what the traffic would bear while eschewing
outright chicanery, and dividing their time with a clear conscience between "Meeting house and Counting house." What
made Logan unique was his absolute control of the Proprietary
Land Office, which in turn controlled the flow of immigrants
into the colony. "Absolute" is not too strong a word to describe
Logan's power; no one but the agent of the proprietor was sanc-
tioned to deal with the Indians about land, and the records of
the Land Office were confidential; neither the Governor appointed by Penn nor the popularly elected Assembly had
access to them. Only the Founder himself could have kept
a tight rein on his provincial agent. But as Penn's problems
in England multiplied, he came to rely more and more on
Logan, who succeeded in concealing from his employer the

extent of his personal involvement in furs and land speculation. Especially after 1712, when Penn suffered the stroke
that incapacitated him until his death in 1718, the temptations
for James Logan must have been very great indeed.

Logan was an astonishingly talented man in many fields. He
was a scholar and a linguist who read Greek, Latin, Hebrew,
Arabic, French, Spanish and Italian, and amassed a library of
more than two thousand volumes (yet unlike Penn, he made no
effort to learn any Indian tongue). He was a scientist who
taught himself mathematics, corresponded with the savants of
the Royal Society, and contributed papers on optics, astronomy,
and botany to the learned journals of Europe. He was a clever
politician who fought against the popular party in the Assembly
in the name of the Proprietary interests (and often, *sub rosa,* in
his own interest as well) and usually won. He was also a moral
philosopher who produced a lengthy treatise called *The Duties
of Man Deduced from Nature,* and who revealed his personal
business ethic in these words: "Should I with open eyes give
away those advantages, that by God's Blessing my own industry
and management have thrown on me, to others who have had
no part in that management, I could never account for it to
my Self and family."

It is impossible to keep track of all the ramifications of Logan's "industry and management," partly because he had so
many fingers in so many different pies, and partly because, as
one contemporary antagonist put it, "No one living knows better
how to puzzle the state of an account." It is safe to say that as a
politician he was a veritable provincial Pooh-Bah, and as a
businessman he functioned as a kind of one-man interlocking di-
rectorate. As Logan the International Merchant, he was able to
finance ventures with risk capital lent to him out of Proprietary
funds by Logan the Proprietary Agent. As Logan the Commis-
sioner of Property, he was able to parcel out what Francis Jen-

44

nings calls an "amazing acreage" to employees of Logan the Indian Trader to be used as bases of operation. When Logan the Provincial Secretary conducted official negotiations with the Indians, he hired the employees of Logan the Indian Trader as interpreters with Proprietary or Provincial funds, and out of these same funds he bought ceremonial presents for the Indians from Logan the International Merchant. And when his own associates got into debt to Logan the Financier, he seized their possessions, including the lands that he had so generously distributed from the otherwise sacrosanct personal estates of the Penn family.

As the flow of European immigrants to the colony increased after 1720, driving up the value of real estate, Logan's attention began to turn more and more from his lucrative position in the fur trade to the even more lucrative opportunities in land speculation. (In 1768 a local squire would look back and comment, "It is almost a proverb in this neighborhood that 'Every great fortune made here within these fifty years has been by land.'") With all his powers—in addition to his other offices, he also served at one time or another as President of the Governor's Council, Chief Justice of the Supreme Court, Receiver of the Proprietary Rents, and Trustee of William Penn's will—Logan's competitive position in the new gold rush was assured. In fact, the only major impediments to his successful conversion of trading posts into real estate tracts were the hunting and trapping Indians who happened to live on the most desirable "undeveloped" land.

Historians agree that when the French and Indian War came to Pennsylvania in 1756, the first blows were struck by members of the Shawnee and Delaware (Lenape) tribes who had moved west to the Ohio Valley to escape the encroachments of white settlers. The Lenape in particular claimed that they had been cheated out of their lands and forced off their reservations, in violation of their well-remembered agreements with the still-revered "Onas" (the Lenape word for "pen"). One of the incidents they sought revenge for is known to history as the Walking Purchase of 1737, and it is often cited as the classic case of fraud perpetrated by white men on the American Indian.

The man primarily responsible for the Walking Purchase was Thomas Penn, the second son of the Founder by his second wife, and a nominal Quaker who later joined the Church of England. His father had left behind him a heavily mortgaged estate and a bitterly contested will; when the terms of the inheritance were finally worked out, Thomas Penn emerged as chief spokesman for the family interest. He arrived in Pennsylvania in 1732 to assume personal control of the Proprietary. It soon became clear, from his conduct in a complicated land deal in Bucks County, that he was determined to disencumber his father's estate by any means at his disposal (even in the face of bitter opposition from the Quaker-controlled Assembly).

According to the provincial charter drawn up by his father, the Proprietary was bound to extinguish all Indian claims to a tract of land *before* offering it for sale to white settlers. But Thomas Penn, strapped for cash, had begun selling some choice tracts in Bucks County, in an area known as the Forks of the Delaware, on the assumption that he could later come to terms with the Indians who lived there. The Indians, a band of Lenape led by a chief named Nutimus, turned out to be less cooperative than expected. When several meetings with Nutimus failed to yield the desired results—either because the Indians refused to sell or because their asking price was too high—Thomas Penn suddenly produced a copy of an old deed which proved, he said, that his father had *already* bought the land in question. According to this piece of paper, Chief Nutimus' forebears had assigned to William Penn, in 1686, all the land that a man could pace off in a day and a half along the riverbank. Apparently, the original "walk" had not been completed, but that was a minor detail that could easily be rectified.

Nutimus and his advisers, however, questioned the validity of the old deed—among other things, Thomas Penn's copy contained no signatures and the all-important *direction* of the walk was not indicated. When the Indians refused to move, the Proprietary forces, increasingly desperate to make good on their promises to the white investors, tried still another stratagem. James Logan dispatched the official provincial interpreter, a man named Conrad Weiser, to see if the sachems of the Iroquois Six Nations could be bribed into "remembering" that they had once conquered the Lenape of the Delaware Valley, which would have meant according to Indian as well as white man's law that Chief Nutimus' people no longer had any right to the land they lived on.

Like most of the Indians of the northeastern woodlands, the Delaware Lenape were allied to the powerful Iroquois Six Nations through a complicated "covenant chain." The Iroquois were the acknowledged leaders of the chain, but the allied tribes had varying degrees of autonomy which were well understood by all parties concerned; and the Lenape had been disposing of land rights for years without a murmur of protest from the Iroquois or anyone else. In fact, according to Weiser's confidential report to Logan, the sachems of the Six Nations at first hesitated "about signing over their right upon the Delaware because they said they had nothing to do there about the land. They were afraid they should do anything amiss to their cousins, the Delawares." But the Iroquois were by now well acquainted with the methods of European diplomacy, and Weiser finally managed to change their minds. In exchange for personal presents ("The charges will be somewhat larger than you most expect," he wrote Logan) and a promise of future diplomatic favors, the Iroquois sachems did agree to betray their "cousins" to the south.

Once this secret bargain had been sealed, Thomas Penn began final preparations for the long-delayed walk. One slight problem was that a day-and-a-half walk under normal circumstances would cover about thirty miles, a distance not quite sufficient for Penn's purposes. So, unknown to the Indians and contrary to accepted custom, a route had already been blazed and cleared through the forest and men noted for their athletic ability (and willingness to keep their mouths shut) had been selected and specially trained. By running instead of walking, and by using horses to carry their provisions, and boats to ferry them across streams, Thomas Penn's hired athletes managed to cover nearly twice the usual mileage in the allotted time. And when the provincial surveyors recorded the results, the lines drawn on paper were extended even farther, until the Indian claims were "extinguished" from all the tracts that Thomas Penn and his brothers (and other speculators including James Logan) had an interest in.

The Indians protested the entire procedure. But white settlers poured in anyway, and within a few years, tensions had increased to such a point that the long-quiescent Lenape began to talk about defending their territorial rights with more than words. Now the Proprietary forces played their trump card. In 1742 a delegation of Iroquois sachems arrived in Philadelphia, and fulfilled the terms of their secret agreement with Weiser by summarily ordering the Delaware Lenape to leave their homeland: "We charge you to remove instantly. We don't give you liberty to think about it," the Iroquois spokesman told Nutimus. The alliance between the Six Nations and the Pennsylvania Proprietary was too powerful to resist. Most of Chief Nutimus' people migrated to the Ohio Valley, in what is now western Pennsylvania, where bitter tales of the white man's duplicity had already become a familiar topic around the council fires.

Quaker apologists have been only too happy to trace the alienation of the Lenape Indians to the Walking Purchase of 1737. It makes a neat dividing line—as long as the Founder or his faithful executors were in charge of Indian policies, the natives were content; when the legacy of the father was undermined by the greed of the apostate son, the natives became restless, and eventually rebellious. And since the mass of good Quakers in Pennsylvania did not hear of the son's fraudulent practices until the damage was done, the most they can be blamed for is lack of vigilance in protecting their Holy Experiment from outside influences. Unfortunately, this simplistic explanation has served only to weaken the pacifist argument, since the record shows that the Indians in Pennsylvania had been the victims of less publicized but equally unsavory land-grabs *before* the arrival of Thomas Penn, and these earlier incidents had involved some of the Province's most prominent business and political leaders (including James Logan).

There is no doubt that greed—in the form of land-hunger— was a major factor in the chain of events that led to the dissolution of the Long Peace. But this chain did not begin with Thomas Penn's activities in 1737. The apostate son only speeded up a process that was at least partly Quaker in origin. "The truth is," writes Frederick Tolles, "there was a conflict implicit in the Quaker ethic insofar as it applied to economic life. On the one hand, Friends were encouraged to be industrious in their callings by the promise that God would add his blessing in the form of prosperity; on the other hand, they were warned against allowing the fruits of their honest labors to accumulate lest they be tempted into luxury and pride." The first generation of

Quaker leaders recognized the problem, but they were also confident that they had the solution. William Penn, as we have seen, counted the enjoyment of property as one of the fundamental rights of Englishmen, and he worked hard to get some enjoyment out of his. At the same time, he could write: "Hardly anything is given us for ourselves, but the Publick may claim a share with us. But of all we call ours, we are most accountable to God and the Publick for our Estates: In this we are but Stewards, and to hoard up all to ourselves is a great injustice as well as ingratitude." For these earliest Quakers, the doctrine of "stewardship" was the essential link between the Puritan ideal of the sanctified individual and the communitarian dream that inspired the Holy Experiment. And their devotion to this doctrine was no mere lip service. Despite his straitened circumstances, Penn turned down a bid of £6,000 from a London syndicate that wanted a monopoly on the Indian trade in the new colony. "I did refuse a great temptation last 2nd day," he wrote to a friend, adding that he would not act in a manner unworthy of Divine Providence—"and so defile what came to me clean."

The contrast between Penn's attitude and the personal business ethic of James Logan, quoted earlier, is especially instructive. Logan died in 1751 at Stenton, his country estate in Germantown, enormously wealthy and full of honors, and with his carefully tended reputation as faithful executor of the Founder's Indian policies intact. As long as this reputation was accepted at face value by most historians (Quaker and non-Quaker), the events leading up to the French and Indian War seemed inexplicable, except by the kind of simplistic formulas offered by the Quaker apologists on one hand, and the anti-Quaker writers of the Boorstin school on the other.

Recently, other historians, working from manuscript sources, have begun to piece together the details of Logan's complex business ventures, and these reveal a very different picture from that presented in the official archives. (Unlike the more impetuous Thomas Penn, Logan had the means and took the time to cover his tracks, at least from the sight of his contemporaries.) During his career, which spanned the first five decades of the eighteenth century, there were Friends who opposed him in the political struggles in Council and Assembly, and there were other Friends who aided in his enterprises and profited by them. Logan was certainly influenced by the Quaker milieu in which he moved; and in comparison with other colonial entrepreneurs in the Indian trade, he moved slowly and with caution. Yet the long-term results of his industry differed hardly at all from the pattern in other colonies.

One of the bitter tales already current among the exiled Indians in the Ohio Valley at the time of the Walking Purchase concerned a band of Lenape who had lived on Brandywine Creek, in what is now Chester County, Pennsylvania. During William Penn's first visit to Pennsylvania, the Brandywine Lenape had sold their interest in the land and received an explicit guarantee from the Proprietary to a reservation along the creek. The first encroachment on this reservation came in 1702, only *four months* after Penn had sailed for England for the last time. While the Indians were absent on one of their periodic hunting and fishing expeditions, a large tract of land along the Brandywine was sold by the Commissioners of Property (now headed by James Logan) to a man named George Harland (who just happened to be a boyhood friend of Logan's, having attended the same Quaker meeting in northern Ireland.) Although both men admitted in private correspondence that the Indians' claim was valid, the land passed into the permanent possession of white settlers. When the angry Indians insisted on being paid for the land they had never intended to surrender, their petitions were supported, curiously enough, by the white settlers themselves. The reason behind this temporary alliance was sim-

51

ple self-interest: the settlers wanted a clear title to their property, and they knew that, under the Charter, only the Commissioners of Property had the legal power to "extinguish" the Indian claims. After four years of on-and-off negotiations, the Commissioners agreed to pay the Brandywine Lenape £100, which was one-third of the sum the Indians had asked for.

The Lenape retreated farther up the creek, where for the next two decades they tried to protect what was left of their reservation (while trying to collect in full the £100 they had been promised). Little by little, white settlers pressed in on the Indians; finally, in 1724, a land speculator began selling tracts directly adjacent to their village. The Brandywine sent a delegation to Philadelphia to protest; fortunately for them, the provincial government at this time was in the hands of a strongly anti-Logan party, headed by Governor William Keith. Keith, an Anglican, was not exactly a friend of the Indian. In fact, just a few years before, he had blatantly violated all the existing Indian treaties by "inviting" a group of German settlers to squat on lands already occupied by another band of Lenape along the Schuylkill River. But it so happened that Keith and Logan had become involved in a power struggle to determine which man would reap the profits from the Schuylkill transaction, and Keith now saw a chance to undermine Logan's position by championing the Brandywine Lenape against the Commissioners of Property.

Although the Governor and his allies had no access to Logan's private papers or to the Land Office records, they were able to interview the petitioning Indians in an open session of the Provincial Assembly. The spokesman for the Brandywine Lenape summed up the Indians' case in these words:

> When William Penn first came to this Country, he settled a perpetual friendship with us; and after we sold him our Country, he reconveyed back a certain Tract of land upon Brandy-wine,

for a Mile on each Side of the said Creek, and to a certain Place up the same Creek, which said Writing was, by the Burning of a Cabin, destroy'd; but we all very well remember the Contents thereof; That William Penn promised that we should not be molested . . . from Generation to Generation; And now it is not Half an Age of an old Man since, and we are molested and our land surveyed out, and settled, before we can reap our Corn off.

What the Indians wanted now was a new piece of paper that spelled out their rights to the land still under their control. The Assembly, led by Keith's supporters, pressed Logan and the other Commissioners to settle the matter, but the speculator, who had already begun "developing" the reservation, balked at any arrangement that would jeopardize his heavy investment. A characteristic "compromise" was worked out. The speculator made a public "Declaration and Promise" that neither he nor his heirs would disturb or molest the Indians, while (unknown to the Indians) the Commissioners of Property gave the speculator a legal document which guaranteed that his "Rights and the Equity thereof shall remain and continue the same . . . as if such Declaration and Promise had never been made . . ."

Within a month, Keith had been replaced by a new governor who allied himself with Logan, and the fate of the Indians was sealed. Before long, a Brandywine chief named Checochinican was complaining to the governor that the Indians' reservation was being surveyed and sold out from under them. For an answer, Checochinican found himself being sued by another associate of Logan in the newly created court of Lancaster County. The court records fail to mention the basis of the suit, but they do give the outcome. Checochinican lost; and neither his name nor that of his band of Lenape is found again in the official ledgers of the province. Presumably, the surviving Brandywines went west, to the banks of the Ohio, like their brethren from the

ON DOING GOOD

Schuylkill a few years before them, and their brethren from the
Delaware a few years after.

The successful career of James Logan (whose half-hearted
Quaker affiliation seems almost symbolic) is a perfect demonstration of how the self-aggrandizing side of the Quaker ethic
came to the fore in Pennsylvania, upsetting the intended balance between individual and communal responsibility. The
spiritual leaders of Philadelphia Yearly Meeting in the latter
part of the eighteenth century—men like John Woolman and
Anthony Benezet—warned repeatedly against this trend toward
an Acquisitive Society. "One would think," Benezet wrote, "by
the general conduct of even the better sort of Friends in matters
of *property*, that some of our Saviour's positive injunctions to his
followers had no meaning." And again: "The appellation of
Steward is what we often take upon ourselves, but indeed in the
mouth of many it is but a cant, unmeaning expression."

By this time, ironically enough, one area of potential conflict
between the humanitarian ideals of the Founder and the economic adventurism of his executors had already been eliminated
in a "peaceful" manner. The virtual removal of the local Indians
had effectively resolved the province's Indian problem. But as
William Penn well knew, the active pacifist can never be satisfied with the merely negative goal of avoiding violence. Because
he believes that no one is safe where anyone is exploited, he
seeks to keep the peace through a comprehensive, imaginative,
unending effort to put humanitarian ideals into practice. Anything less than this he regards as not only immoral but unrealistic. The final decade of Quaker rule in Pennsylvania may be
taken as an illustration of what happens when this precept is ignored.

In his detailed summary of Indian-European relations in colonial Pennsylvania, Francis Jennings ventures this generalization:

54

One outstanding fact of the Long Peace is that the Indians were only gradually, over the entire period, reduced to the state of objects; they were never conceived as expendable weapons of war to be flung against each other or against other Europeans. *If there is one simple reason for the Long Peace, it is just that the Pennsylvanians never launched war—against anyone.* If there is one simple reason for the end of the Long Peace, it is just that the Pennsylvanians became so indifferent to the human needs of the Indians that the natives were obliged to get their necessities from other people who did launch wars. The province became an arena when it became a place that Indians refuged *from* instead of *to.* [Emphasis added.]

The Lenape and Shawnee Indians who left Pennsylvania for exile in the West thought that they had found a refuge in the Ohio Valley from the white man's land-hunger. But by 1750, the Ohio Valley itself had become the next great prize for the rival trading interests, land speculators, and empire-builders from French Canada and the English colonies of Pennsylvania, Maryland, Virginia, and New York. The rapidly worsening plight of the exiles (who now formed a fairly cohesive community known as the Ohio Indians) was best expressed by a Lenape interpreter who asked one of the white entrepreneurs "where the Indian's land lay, for that the French claimed all the Land on one Side [of] the River Ohio and the English on the other Side."

When the French decided to back up their claim to the Ohio Valley by driving out the English traders with an armed expedition, the Indians had no choice except to ally themselves with the French; they were so dependent on trade that the alternative for them was, literally, starvation. But despite the establishment of a French military presence at Fort Duquesne (where Pittsburgh stands today), the Ohio Indians were not at all eager to fight the English. There may have been a number of reasons. For one thing, the Indians still preferred English trade goods—

55

and English prices—to those offered by the French. In addition, fighting the English meant fighting the Pennsylvanians, and the memories of better days under William Penn were still very much alive. The promises had been broken, but the old men of the Lenape and Shawnee still passed down detailed accounts of the famous treaties that had been negotiated as if between equals. It was known that Quakers still controlled the Pennsylvania Assembly (although they had been a minority in the province since the early 1700's) and the very word "Quaker" commanded great respect in Indian councils. Down through the years, relations had continued to be friendly with individual Quaker farmers, who were apparently a rarity among European colonists—they displayed interest in the natives as human beings without trying to convert them to a new religion.

Whatever their exact motives, it is worth noting that at least some of the Indians in the Ohio Valley did their best to stay out of the impending French-English conflict—even though they were clients of the French at the time. For instance, they did nothing to resist a military probe sent out by Virginia in May of 1754 under the command of a twenty-two-year-old colonel named George Washington. They also showed no inclination to fight *alongside* the inexperienced Virginian, even after he grandly announced that the English had come "to put you again in possession of your lands, and to take care of your wives and children, to dispossess the French, to maintain your rights and to secure the whole country for you." (The Indians' skepticism may have been reinforced by young Washington's manner, which by all accounts was overbearing in the best Virginian tradition.)

When Washington's column was soundly defeated by the French a few weeks later, His Majesty's government in London decided that the time had come to commit the main forces of the Empire to defend the western frontier (and incidentally, to secure the investments of influential men on both sides of the Atlantic). An army of 1,400 British regulars was dispatched, under the command of General Edward Braddock. From the point of view of the Ohio Indians, this English decision promised to restore the local balance of power between the two European empires, which meant that the Indians would once again be able to place themselves under the protector of their choice. As Braddock's men were literally hacking their way through the wilderness toward Fort Duquesne, a delegation of Indians led by a Lenape chief named Shingas came to powwow with the English commander about renewing the old alliance. Before committing themselves in the imminent battle, however, the Indians wanted some further assurance about what would happen to the land once the French were defeated. According to an account of the interview dictated by Shingas and recorded by a white Pennsylvanian, General Braddock replied bluntly that when the French had been defeated, "The English should inhabit and inherit the land." Shingas then asked "Whether the Indians that were Friends to the English might not be permitted to Live and Trade among the English and have Hunting Ground sufficient to support themselves and Families as they had nowhere to Flee but into the Hands of the French and their Indians who were their Enemies (that is, Shingas' Enemies)." Braddock refused to make any concessions, saying that he did not need the help of the Lenape and Shawnee to drive away the French. After virtually begging him to change his mind, Shingas finally told the English commander that if the Indians "might not have the Liberty to live on the land, they would not fight for it." This was in May of 1755. Two months later, while the Ohio Indians looked on in sullen neutrality, Braddock's army was ambushed and cut to pieces by a much smaller force of Frenchmen and their Canadian Indian allies. Braddock died of his wounds a few hours after the battle, murmuring, according to one report, "We shall know better how to deal with them next time."

The destruction of Braddock's army left the French supreme in the Ohio Valley, and what the French wanted was simply to see every trace of the English scoured from the region. Even those Lenape who might have preferred to maintain their neutrality between the two empires were hardly willing to starve for the privilege of not fighting. And if there was ever a time for settling a few old scores, this was it.

When widespread Indian raids began in western Pennsylvania in the winter of 1755–56, the brunt of the attacks was borne not by Quakers—who were settled only sparsely in the backwoods—but by settlers of Scotch-Irish origin and Presbyterian persuasion. James Logan, a fellow countryman, had been largely responsible for their immigration in the preceding decades. The Scotch-Irish were famous for their short tempers and fighting prowess, and Logan had written candidly to one of William Penn's sons that it might be prudent to "plant" these Ulstermen on the Susquehanna "as a frontier in case of any disturbance . . ." He did not mention that he stood to make a lot of money out of planting them. Nor did the avowed exponent of defensive war seem to mind that the views of the Scotch-Irish Presbyterians were diametrically opposed to those of the late Founder on the Indian question; as Logan noted, the Bible-quoting Ulstermen felt that it was "against the laws of God and Nature that so much land should lie idle while so many Christians wanted it to labor on and raise their bread." He must also have known that such settlers would not be deterred by the fact that most of the land which looked so invitingly idle was actually part of the traditional hunting and fishing preserves of one or another of the neighboring tribes of heathen.

Now that the Indians were on the warpath in the west, the anti-Quaker forces of the Proprietary (controlled from behind the scenes by Thomas Penn) led a public outcry for the Assembly in Philadelphia to take action to protect the "innocent" settlers. It was common knowledge that nothing in Quaker doctrine commanded Friends to stand in the way of *other* people arming themselves. The majority Quaker view had been stated many times in the Assembly: "While we do not as the world is now circumstanced condemn the use of arms in others, we are principled against bearing arms ourselves." The real issue was whether the Quaker Assemblymen would loosen the provincial purse-strings sufficiently to allow the non-Quaker governor, Robert Morris, to put the colony on a war footing. On a number of occasions in the past, the Assembly had bowed to political pressures, and had voted funds for British military expeditions *outside* the province, earmarking the money ambiguously "for the King's use." There was great hesitancy among the Quaker legislators to apply this dubious precedent *within* the province, but at the end of 1755 the Assembly did vote another £60,000 for the "King's use," and passed a bill authorizing the creation of a citizen's militia to be manned through voluntary enlistment, with Quakers and other conscientious objectors specifically excused. At the same time, the leading members of the Society of Friends decided to launch an investigation of their own into the chances for a negotiated peace; they still could not bring themselves to believe that their old friends, the Leni-Lenape, were committing the reported atrocities on the frontier.

Neither the limited militia bill nor the private peace initiative pleased the Proprietary, and in April, 1756, Governor Morris and his executive council officially declared war on the Lenape and Shawnee Indians (without consulting the Assembly). To ensure the widest possible participation in the struggle to save Christian civilization from the "cruel and barbarous" savages, cash bounties were offered for fresh Indian scalps: $130 for a male over twelve years of age and $50 for a female. Many of the Quaker Assemblymen, who had been returned to their seats in the last election by a largely non-Quaker electorate, now found it impossible to serve in a wartime government. Even those legislators who might have been tempted to remain in office to restrain the war hawks and bounty-hunters were under great pressure from another quarter. As a result of Thomas Penn's machinations in London, the British government was considering a proposal to impose a loyalty oath as a qualification for membership in all colonial assemblies, an act which would have permanently barred Friends from holding elective office in the New World. Influential English Quakers managed to work out a last minute political compromise: The general loyalty oath proposal would be dropped if the Quaker legislators in Pennsylvania resigned, at least for the duration of the military emergency. The patriarchs of Philadelphia Yearly Meeting reluctantly agreed; and control of the Pennsylvania Assembly passed to the political followers of Benjamin Franklin.

Historians usually date the end of the Holy Experiment from the mass resignation of the Quaker Assemblymen. As neat as this chronology might sound, it leaves out one of the most important chapters of the story. When the Quakers resigned from the legislature, they redoubled their efforts, as private citizens, on behalf of the newly organized "Friendly Association for Regaining and Preserving Peace with the Indians by Pacific Measures."

By the end of the year, the following appraisal of the situation in Pennsylvania from the Friendly point of view had been dispatched to London Yearly Meeting:

> Some of the Indians in the Interest of the French having committed hostilities on the Frontiers . . . the Consideration of the Circumstances of those Indians who had been our old Friends and Neighbors led some of us to think whether we, as a Society in Particular and this Government in general, had fully discharged our duty to them. A little Reflection was Sufficient

to convince us that there had been a Deficiency, and incited to
a Concern to give them some fresh Testimony of our regard,
which some of us in our private Stations were willing to Manifest, and Others by their endeavours to engage the Government
to do it in Such manner as would be more immediately Effec-
tual.

Nothing could have been better calculated to infuriate the
hawks of the day than such soul-searching on the part of well-
to-do merchants who were being asked to contribute not their
lives but only their purses to the war effort. While mighty empires moved inexorably toward a showdown along the frontier,
the Quakers were examining their consciences! To a historian
like Daniel Boorstin, the Quaker peace initiatives amount to
"meddling" and "tampering" on the part of idealists who were so
blinded by "moral slogans or abstract principles" that they
could not see clearly the "character of the Indian problem"—as,
for instance, Governor Morris could. Even Quaker-oriented historians tend to find a certain naïveté in the Quakers' appraisal of
the *casus belli,* and their suggestions for removing it. Yet the
Quakers were not talking about stopping the French muskets
and Indian tomahawks with love. They were talking quite specifically about the reasons behind the change in allegiance of
the Lenape Indians—an event which competent military com-
manders on all sides agreed was a matter of strategic importance. And in examining their consciences, the "impractical"
Quakers appear to have struck closer to the truth—as belatedly
disclosed in the private papers of James Logan and his
confederates—than any of their more worldly critics.

Having heard that the Indians of Pennsylvania had been
alienated by unfair treatment, the Quaker leaders decided to
find out for themselves whether there was any basis to the Indian grievances, and if so, whether these grievances could be re-
dressed to the Indians' satisfaction. Led by Israel Pemberton, a

prominent Philadelphia merchant, the Friendly Association got in touch with an Indian chief named Tedyuscung, the acknowledged spokesman for the handful of Lenape who had chosen to remain in Pennsylvania rather than migrate west. A conference was arranged at Easton, in the Forks of the Delaware, where Tedyuscung told the Pennsylvania authorities that the Indians were fighting because their land had been taken from them by fraud—and he stamped his foot to indicate that the very ground on which they sat had been a part of the booty. The Proprietary officials dismissed Tedyuscung as a notorious drunk (he was said to have a capacity for up to a gallon of rum a day), and refused to let anyone examine the pertinent Council minutes and Land Office records. But a temporary truce was negotiated with the Indians under Tedyuscung's control, and a second powwow was scheduled for the following spring.°

Meanwhile, the Quakers' private inquiry into the causes of the hostilities continued. One of the investigators was William Logan, the son of James but a much better Quaker than his father. After delving into the family archives, he was apparently deeply disturbed to learn something about his father's involvement in the earlier land speculations. Even for the son, however, the true picture of James Logan's multifarious operations was impossible to piece together while most of the relevant papers were locked away in other people's desk drawers, or otherwise protected from public scrutiny. The records of the Land Office were finally seized and copied by the Assembly in 1759, but by that time much of the corroboratory evidence had simply disap-

---

° Negotiations with the Indians were invariably lengthy, precisely because the "control" of the chiefs was a tenuous thing; although the white men referred to them in terms appropriate to European sovereigns—"King Philip," "King Shingas"—the chiefs were often no more than respected advisers, "first among equals," whose power lay not in divine right but in eloquence and persuasiveness.

peared. Historians have recently discovered that the numerous distortions and gaps in the records can only be corrected by comparing the official documents with the private letters and ledgers of the men involved. Because of the fragmentary nature of the evidence available—and also, no doubt, because of a reluctance to expose their own dirty linen in public—the Quaker investigators focused on the more blatant fraud of the Walking Purchase, and on Thomas Penn's unmistakable role in it.

The Quakers, however, did more than just try to fix the blame for the alienation of the Indians. At the second powwow, in the spring of 1757, the truce with Tedyuscung's people was confirmed. This agreement was not of major importance in itself, since the real trouble was with the Lenape who had migrated to the Ohio Valley. But the treatment accorded to Tedyuscung was one way of letting the Ohio Indians know that Pennsylvania, under the prodding of the Friendly Association and the Franklinists, was now willing to talk peace.

A major Indian conference was called for Philadelphia in 1758. Among the dignitaries who attended were representatives of the Iroquois Six Nations, the British Crown, the colonies of New York, New Jersey and Pennsylvania, and both the eastern and western Lenape. As their spokesman, the western Lenape sent a chief named Pisquetomen, a brother of Shingas, and a man who had good reason to be wary in dealing with both white and red men. He had been living along the Schuylkill River when the German squatters overran the Indian lands, and he had been Chief Nutimus' interpreter at the Walking Purchase negotiations and at the subsequent meeting when the Iroquois humiliated the Delaware Lenape and ordered them from their homes. Yet he retained an affection for the Quakers. After some hard bargaining at Philadelphia, he agreed to convey to his people the terms of a proposed settlement, which included amnesty for the Indian warriors who had attacked the province, a guarded admission that the Indian claims to land in Pennsylvania had not been properly extinguished, and a promise (backed by the Crown) that there would be *no more white immigration beyond the Appalachians.*

These terms proved to be acceptable to the Ohio Indians, who subsequently withdrew from their alliance with the French. This withdrawal, in turn, prompted the French abandonment of Fort Duquesne without a fight, before a new British expeditionary force under the command of General John Forbes could arrive. Whether the strength of Forbes's expedition would have frightened the Indians back into neutrality even without the Quaker initiative is a moot point (especially with the Braddock fiasco still fresh in their minds). But General Forbes, a much more flexible man than Braddock, was intensely aware of the importance of Indian allies in the overall military picture; far from considering the work of the Friendly Association "naïve" or "meddling," he corresponded at length with Israel Pemberton about the basic issues, and sent his own representative to talk peace to the Indians of the Ohio Valley.

Many members of the Friendly Association had refused to pay war taxes during the emergency as a matter of conscience. Now they took up a collection among their coreligionists to underwrite the entire cost of the peace treaty. With the negotiations dragging on for several more years, the final settlement, including a long-delayed compensation for Chief Nutimus' people, came to approximately £5,000.

The conclusion of the peace treaty did not signify any letup in the polemical battle to assign responsibility for the tragic events along the Pennsylvania frontier. Daniel Boorstin was only taking his place in the mainstream of American scholarship when he portrayed the frontier as reaping "the fiery harvest of a half-century of Quaker generosity and non-resistance to the Indians." The familiar assumptions about American Indians that

underlie Boorstin's pages can be found in more explicit detail in
the works of Francis Parkman, the nineteenth-century historian
who has remained the single most influential interpreter of the
events surrounding the French and Indian War. Parkman's attitude toward the clash of cultures on the American frontier may
be surmised from this statement in his two-volume *History of
the Conspiracy of Pontiac,* published in 1851:

> To reclaim the Indians from their savage state has again and
> again been attempted, and each attempt has failed. Their in-
> tractable, unchanging character leaves no other alternative than
> their gradual extinction or the abandonment of the western
> world to eternal barbarism.

Yet Parkman wrote with such high style and seeming authority
that the "objective" part of his work was considered above re-
proach for more than half a century. In the last few years, scholars like Francis Jennings have begun to show how Parkman's
anti-Indian bias led him into systematic distortions of his
sources—distortions that sometimes disguised the role that the
Indians played in their own history, and that tended to sub-
merge any hint whatever of rational motivation for Indian behavior. When Parkman's sources are re-examined, the picture of
the American Indian that emerges is somewhat closer to the assumptions on which the Quaker patriarchs in Pennsylvania operated.

The leaders of the Friendly Association insisted that the Indians were not on a senseless rampage, but were at least partly
seeking to avenge themselves against people who had seized
their lands by fraud or brute force. To support this contention,
the Quakers pointed out that members of the Friends—whom
the Indians considered, rightly or wrongly, as fair dealers in
land—had been almost entirely spared during the outbreak.
Writing in December of 1758, Israel Pemberton asked:

> Is it not a consequence worthy of thankful remembrance, that in all the desolation on our frontiers, not one Friend we have heard of has been slain or carried captive, and we have reason to think, both from their [i.e. the Indians'] conduct in places where Friends were as much exposed as others and from their declarations to us, they would never hurt Friends if they knew us to be such.

A few years later, one of the Shawnees who had taken part in the raids on Pennsylvania independently confirmed this assertion; the warrior was recorded as saying that the Indians were able to recognize the Quakers "by the simplicity of [their] appearance which in times of war had been a preservation to [them]." Even the "massacres" of 1756—horrible as they were, as all war is—indicate that the Indians had something on their minds other than random blood-letting. The first raid on Pennsylvania, led by Pisquetomen himself, was directed against the home of Conrad Weiser, the Indian agent, who was living in the Schuylkill Valley on land that had been seized from Pisquetomen's own people. And while Israel Pemberton was mistaken in asserting that the handful of Quaker backwoodsmen were totally exempt from Indian attacks, the one verified exception may be said to prove the rule: The Indians did mount an attack on the home of Edward Marshall, a Quaker who was one of the three "walkers" in the Walking Purchase of 1737.

In this matter, as in so many other questions concerning the American frontier, the variable introduced by Indian illiteracy makes any final judgment especially hazardous. Quakers like Pemberton may have misjudged the character of the Indians. They may even have been deluded in their belief that decency and savagery were to be found on both sides of the frontier, and that it was worth appealing to the decency in an effort to ameliorate the savagery. But whether or not the Friendly Association's assumptions about the Indians were correct, there seems to be little doubt that most other American colonists considered them to be *subversive*. It was no coincidence that the same Quakers who refused to take sides in the war between white men and red men also opposed the enslavement of black men. In each case, the Quaker belief that there is "that of God in every one" ran directly counter to the emerging colonial ideology—an ideology which hung a "white only" sign on the sacred rights of Private Property, Personal Liberty, the Pursuit of Happiness, and often Life itself.°

Still, it is one thing for a man to have a moral insight, and another for him to apply it rigorously and consistently to every aspect of his life and to the society around him as well. One of the few American Friends to approach this ideal was John Woolman, who holds a place in the informal hagiology of Quakerism just below that of George Fox and William Penn. Woolman was the antithesis of James Logan in almost every way, not the least important being his explicit recognition that the real danger to the Holy Experiment lay in an unholy colonial alliance of racism, militarism, and economic exploitation.

Woolman was born in 1720 on a farm in Rancocas, Burlington County, New Jersey, where his formal education began, and ended, at the local Quaker schoolhouse. He was then apprenticed to a shopkeeper and tailor, and later opened a retail shop of his own in the town of Mount Holly. His business prospered,

---

° The power of a racist ideology to dehumanize both its adherents and its opponents—and thereby make it possible for ordinary men to perform otherwise inconceivable acts—is familiar enough in the twentieth century. But we have trouble recognizing such a cause-and-effect relationship in our own glorified past. During Pontiac's Rebellion in 1762, a large Indian force laid siege to Fort Pitt for four months; following one of the inconclusive peace powwows between defenders and besiegers—a common feature of Indian wars—an English officer made this entry in his diary: "We gave them 2 Blankets and one Handkerchief out of the Small Pox Hospital. I hope it will have the desired effect . . ."

but instead of deriving satisfaction from his material success, he became uneasy, since the more time he spent in trade, the less time he had for spiritual concerns. Woolman explained the course of action that he took to resolve this dilemma, in an often-quoted entry from his *Journal* (which has become, like George Fox's, a religious classic):

> The increase of business became my burden; for though my natural inclination was towards merchandise, yet I believed Truth required me to live more free from outward cumbers; and there was now a strife in my mind between the two. In this exercise my prayers were put up to the Lord, who graciously heard me, and gave me a heart resigned to his holy will. Then I lessened my outward business, and, as I had opportunity, told my customers of my intentions, that they might consider what shop to turn to; and in a while I wholly laid down merchandise, and followed my trade as a tailor by myself, having no apprentice. I also had a nursery of apple-trees, in which I employed some of my time in hoeing, grafting, trimming, and inoculating.

There is something irresistibly "American" about the mysticism of this reluctant merchant prince. Given Woolman's dilemma, what could be more practical than the terms of his appeal to Holy Will, and the prudent revelation that he received and acted on? His God was not an enemy of profit or private enterprise *per se,* but of the excesses of commerce that went hand in hand with the love of luxury and the desire for wealth and power at any cost. These excesses provided a major theme for Woolman's ministry, whose purpose was not to mortify the flesh but to fortify the conscience.

Typically, his own conscience burned at the recollection that as a young man he had once executed a bill of sale for his employer, in which the item of merchandise was a young Negro woman. Spurred by his own complicity in such evil, he eventually became the leading spirit in the struggle against slaveholding within the Society of Friends. As early as 1688 a Quaker meeting in Germantown had gone on record against involuntary servitude: "There is a liberty of conscience here which is right and reasonable, and there ought to be likewise liberty of the body." By 1696 Philadelphia Yearly Meeting was advising Friends to take no part in the slave trade; and in 1711, the Quaker-led Assembly passed a prohibitive duty on imported slaves (which was annulled by Her Majesty's government in London). But there were also wealthy Quakers (in Pennsylvania and New Jersey as well as the southern colonies) who resisted the pressures to free their slaves, protesting that they treated their Negroes according to the most enlightened principles of Christian ethics. In 1758, at the prompting of Woolman and Anthony Benezet, Philadelphia Yearly Meeting established a committee to "labor with" any Friends in America who still owned slaves; the goal was not merely manumission, but also fair compensation for the years of involuntary servitude. The achievement of this goal, for which Woolman labored tirelessly, took two decades. In the end, a handful of recalcitrants had to be disowned by their monthly meetings. But by 1787—the year the American Constitutional Convention agreed to define a Negro slave as three-fifths of a person for the purpose of census enumeration—the Society of Friends had cleansed itself of slaveholding, and Quakers were free to assume a major role in the formation of a national abolition movement.

Although he is far better known for his successful antislavery efforts, Woolman's persistent advocacy of Indian rights was in a sense the more radical position to his contemporaries, since it was primarily the well-to-do who benefited from the slave system, whereas the Indian lands were a great temptation to wealthy speculator and penniless homesteader alike. At a time when their enemies were claiming that Quakers were incapable of governing because they were too rigidly bound to their ideals, Woolman was insisting that the trouble in Pennsylvania stemmed precisely from the Quakers' failure to live up to their ideals in the face of such temptations.

It was probably inevitable that John Woolman's specific economic critique of the Holy Experiment would be accepted in this country—by both anti-Quaker and Quaker-oriented historians—as evidence of his mystical, perfectionist turn of mind. What he had to say about the society that was taking shape on the North American continent was precisely what that society did not want to hear. Certainly, his rhetoric can be reminiscent of the Old Testament prophets, as in the essay, "A Plea for the Poor," written in 1763 (but not published until thirty years later):

> The rising up of a desire to obtain wealth is the beginning; this desire being cherished, moves to action; and riches thus gotten please self; and while self has a life in them it desires to have them defended. Wealth is attended with Power, by which bargains and proceedings contrary to Universal Righteousness are supported . . . O that we who declare against wars, and acknowledge our trust to be in God only, may walk in the light, and therein examine our foundation and motives in holding great estates! May we look upon our treasures, the furniture of our houses, and our garments, and try whether the seeds of war have nourishment in these our possessions.

The connection between such Biblical cadences and the actual clash of imperial armies, trading blocs, land speculators, and rival ideologies may not be immediately clear (although it hardly takes much imagination to make the leap; in 1897, "A Plea for the Poor" was reprinted in England as a socialist tract by the newly organized Fabian Society). But Woolman also recorded in his *Journal* some of the firsthand experiences that shaped his Christian radicalism, and there can be no mistaking either his excellence as a reporter or his sure grasp of the basic issues. For example, during a journey through western Pennsylvania which he undertook at the height of Pontiac's Rebellion, he had a conversation with an old-time Indian trader which prompted this train of thought:

> I perceived that many white people often sell rum to the Indians, which I believe is a great evil. In the first place, they are thereby deprived of the use of reason, and their spirits being violently agitated, quarrels often arise which end in mischief, and the bitterness and resentment occasioned hereby are frequently of long continuance. Again their skins and furs, gotten through much fatigue and hard travels, with which they intended to buy clothing, they often sell at a low rate for more rum when they become intoxicated; and afterward, when they suffer for want of the necessaries of life, are angry with those who, for the sake of gain, took advantage of their weakness. Their chiefs have often complained of this in their treaties with the English.

As Woolman himself noted, he was not the first white man to recognize this evil. For almost a century Philadelphia Yearly Meeting had been advising Friends not to sell or give liquors to the Indians ("because they use them not to moderation but to Excess and Drunkenness"). But Woolman's analysis of what might be called the "surplus value" of the rum that the white traders were so eager to supply their Indian customers is unusually lucid. And instead of satisfying himself with a stock denunciation of the traders' greed, he proceeded, after further contemplation, to this insight:

> I also remembered that the [white] people on the frontiers, among whom this evil is too common, are often poor; and that they venture to the outside of a colony in order to live more independently of the wealthy, who often set high rents on their land. I was renewedly confirmed in a belief, that if all our inhabitants lived according to sound wisdom, laboring to promote universal love and righteousness, and ceased from every inordinate desire after wealth, and from all customs which are tinctured with luxury, the way would be easy for our inhabitants,

though they might be much more numerous than at present, to live comfortably on honest employments, without the temptation they are so often under of being drawn into schemes to make settlements on lands which have not been purchased of the Indians, or of applying to that wicked practice of selling rum to them.

A few days later, as he penetrated deeper and deeper into Indian country, he tried to sum up his understanding of the social ills that had brought William Penn's great dream to an end:

The sun appearing, we set forward, and as I rode over the barren hills my meditations were on the alterations in the circumstances of the natives of this land since the coming in of the English. The lands near the sea are conveniently situated for fishing; the lands near the rivers, where the tides flow, and some above, are in many places fertile, and not mountainous, while the changing of the tides makes passing up and down easy with any kind of traffic. The natives have in some places, for trifling considerations, sold their inheritance so favourably situated, and in other places have been driven back by superior force; their way of clothing themselves is also altered from what it was, and they being far removed from us have to pass over mountains, swamps and barren deserts, so that travelling is very troublesome in bringing their skins and furs to trade with us. By the extension of English settlements, and partly by the increase of English hunters, the wild beasts on which the natives chiefly depend for subsistence are not so plentiful as they were . . . I had a prospect of the English along the coast for upwards of nine hundred miles, where I travelled, and their favourable situation and the difficulties attending the natives as well as the negroes in many places were open before me . . . And here luxury and covetousness, with the numerous oppressions and other evils attending them, appeared very afflicting to me, and I felt . . . that the seeds of great calamity and desolation are sown and growing fast on this continent.

There seems to be a special significance in the fact that a standard American reference work like the *Dictionary of American Biography* pays homage to Woolman's lifelong struggle against racism, avarice and war in these words: "It was his other-worldliness in thought and deed that was to distinguish him." Wherever Woolman's other-worldliness lay, it could not have been in his conviction that the causes of war and the "inordinate desire after wealth" were intimately bound up together. James Logan, whom no one has ever called other-worldly, happened to share Woolman's views on this point. In a letter supporting Benjamin Franklin's proposal for a voluntary militia in Pennsylvania (1747), Logan wrote: "Our Friends spare no pains to get and accumulate estates, and are yet against defending them, though these very estates are in a great measure the sole cause of their being invaded." The difference between the two men is that, having come to the same insight, Woolman saw no alternative to eschewing wealth (which did *not* mean embracing poverty), while Logan insisted on accumulating wealth (even at the risk of war). Logan's position is, of course, the "realistic" one, and the *Dictionary of American Biography* pays homage to his career in these words: "*Apart from his official duties,* he made a fortune in land investment, and in trade with the Indians." (Emphasis added.)

The lessons to be learned from the Holy Experiment are undoubtedly complex. But one fact stands out: If it was *not* the internal contradictions of a pacifist state that led to the outbreak of hostilities in 1756, if there *is* another cogent explanation for the end of the Long Peace on the Pennsylvania frontier, then the potential for nonviolent initiatives in domestic and international affairs may be far greater than most politicians and historians have been willing to admit.

In a famous prophetic passage on the problems of constitutional government, William Penn observed:

ON DOING GOOD

> . . . Governments rather depend on men, than men upon governments. Let men be good, and the government cannot be bad; if it be ill, they will cure it. But, if men be bad, let the government be never so good, they will endeavour to warp and spoil it to their turn.

It is doubly ironic that Penn, whose genius was in devising political instruments and whose great failure was in misjudging the character of his subordinates, should have provided such a concise summary of John Woolman's social concerns. Throughout his career, Woolman thought in terms of improving men, not institutions. He appealed to men to *make themselves* better, and he was most effective in face-to-face encounters with individual slaveholders. But his efforts to promote "universal love and righteousness" were, in one sense, self-defeating. Although he saw more clearly than any other Quaker leader the dangerous interaction between wealth and power, he was unable to do for the Quaker economic ethic what Penn had done in the political sphere—that is, devise models for social institutions that would reinforce tendencies toward communal responsibility, and discourage or redirect (nonviolently, of course) the selfish impulses that can tear a community apart. In the absence of such models, his critique of the evils in society could easily be taken as a critique of society itself—and as a foreshadowing of the almost complete withdrawal of American Friends from public life in the nineteenth century, in an effort to preserve what they saw as their own purity.

A century later, in an age when withdrawal is no longer conceivable, John Woolman's "other-worldliness" stands as both a warning and a challenge. Any society that tolerates the inequities that he witnessed contains within itself the seeds of destruction. But the private and public institutions that will make it possible for imperfect men to govern equitably in a prosperous community remained to be created.

PART II

CASES

❖ ❖ ❖

A COMMON CONCEPT OF JUSTICE

ONE scorching weekday afternoon in the middle of one of the long hot summers of the late 1960's, a meeting was called at Our Lady of Sorrows Church on the West Side of Chicago. The purpose of the meeting was to bring together a representative of the American Jewish Congress and the officers of the East Garfield Park Tenants Union. The topic for discussion: rebuilding the local black ghetto.

East Garfield Park is a comparatively recent addition to Chicago's slum ghettos. In 1940, its population of 65,789 was ninety-five percent white; in 1960, with a population roughly the same size, it was ninety-eight percent black. The streets near the church are lined with three-story brick houses, built for the rapidly expanding white middle class before the turn of the century; the façades still radiate an air of drab respectability. The entire section was laid out on a strict grid pattern, with broad boulevards and wide sidewalks. At intervals along the curbs unpaved rectangles were left for shade trees. The trees are long gone; the rectangular depressions of bare earth are filled with broken glass. Here and there along the boulevards, the rows of houses are interrupted by empty lots, overgrown with weeds and bearing large white billboards with this inscription: "Progress for East Garfield. A building formerly on this site has been removed by the CITY OF CHICAGO to improve this community. Richard J. Daley, Mayor."

On the morning of the scheduled meeting, Mrs. Minnie Dunlap, the program director of the Tenants Union, had taken the

man from the American Jewish Congress on a tour of some dilapidated apartment buildings on the corner of West Madison
and Albany streets (a few blocks from the center of the local
business district that had been partly burned out in the riots
that spring). The landlord of the dilapidated buildings had
signed a collective-bargaining agreement with the Union a few
months before, but the tenants had recently begun withholding
their rent, after deciding that the landlord was not living up to
the terms of the contract. Their grievances included, in Mrs.
Dunlap's words, "No paint, no locks on the doors, garbage pil-
ing up, plaster falling everywhere, and rats galore."

Now the Tenants Union was thinking about buying the buildings, renovating them, and turning them into low-cost coopera-
tives or condominiums for the present occupants. The landlord,
who was getting no return on his investment as long as the rent
strike continued, was supposedly willing to sell. The American
Jewish Congress had expressed an interest in providing seed
money for the project.

The meeting got off to a late start because the door to Our
Lady of Sorrows Parish Hall was locked and no one could find a
key. In addition to Mrs. Dunlap and the man from the American
Jewish Congress, the conferees were Mrs. Vernedia White, president of the Tenants Union; Mrs. Rosemary Hollins, a tenant organizer; several young white lawyers, volunteers from the Community Legal Services Project; and Tony Henry and Major
Beverly, staff members of the American Friends Service Committee which had guided the Tenants Union through its organizational birth pains and was still supplying advice and financial
support. Some of the volunteer lawyers were familiar figures to
Mrs. White and Mrs. Dunlap; they had defended community
people in numerous eviction cases and had helped draft the contracts with the handful of landlords who had so far agreed to
bargain with the Tenants Union. But one of the attorneys was

new. He was introduced to the Union officers as Daniel Epstein, of the firm of Schradzke, Gould and Ratner, a specialist in the complex field of housing law. Mrs. White stared at him coolly. "You any relation to Epstein Realty Company?" she asked.

Attorney Epstein vigorously denied any connection with the firm that had recently been taken to court by the Tenants Union for a long list of building-code violations.

Everyone laughed, including Mrs. White. Then she looked the young attorney over a second time: "You *sure* you're no kin of Epstein?" There was a painful pause, then everyone laughed again, and on that note, the meeting got down to business.

The man from the American Jewish Congress began by reaffirming his organization's interest in cosponsoring any redevelopment plan that the community found desirable and feasible. The important thing, he stressed, was that the community do its *own* planning. The young attorneys hastened to agree: "We'll find the architects, the consultants, the legal help—whatever you need," one of them said. "The money is available through federal programs. The community just has to sit down and decide what it wants."

But before making such a decision, of course, the people in the community had to be sure that they understood all the different options—and the young attorneys launched into a lengthy discussion of the pros and cons of rehabilitation, new construction, co-ops, rentals, condominiums, high-rises, town houses, walkups, H.U.D. assistance, F.H.A. approval, G.N.M.A. financing, mortgage subsidies, nonprofit sponsors, and so on. One fact that emerged from the tangle of figures and regulations and federalese was that it would definitely be cheaper to demolish and build from the ground up than to rehabilitate buildings as far gone as those at West Madison and Albany. "What we *should* do," one of the lawyers said, warming to the subject, "is burn the whole ghetto down and start over."

79

"If you burn those buildings down, where the people gonna go?" Mrs. Dunlap asked. "We're doubling up already."

With evident reluctance, the lawyers agreed to focus their attention on rehabilitation. According to the most reliable estimates, it appeared to be possible to buy one of the buildings on Albany Street, renovate the interior, and maintain it as a condominium at a cost to each tenant of approximately $125 month.

Mrs. Dunlap shook her head. "The tenants in that building are paying $75 and $100, not $125," she said.

"We could ask if they want new bathrooms," one lawyer said. "If they don't, it could be done for something close to $100."

"They would want new bathrooms," Mrs. Dunlap said firmly.

Attorney Epstein explained that as far as F.H.A. regulations were concerned, it made much better sense to plan for an entire block rather than just a single house. He suggested that the community think bigger. "It's much more efficient; you have to do the same amount of paperwork for one building as you would for many buildings." The most efficient type of construction, he added, would be a full city block of six-story apartment buildings with elevators.

Mrs. Dunlap immediately objected to the elevators. "They have elevators in public housing, and they're constantly getting out of fix."

"If the people owned their own building, they might feel different about keeping it up," Attorney Epstein suggested.

Mrs. Dunlap looked unconvinced. Mrs. White tried to explain: "The thing is, we have some people who want condominiums, some want high-rise, some want to buy their own town houses. For me, I'd like to have a whole town house with some grass around it."

Tony Henry, one of the Service Committee representatives who had been sitting quietly at the far end of the conference table, stood up now and went to a green blackboard against one wall of the room. With a piece of yellow chalk, he drew a large square to represent a city block; then he filled in the big square with a series of smaller squares, to show that the construction of single-family town houses with individual lots would mean fewer families per block than there were at present, which would mean more doubling up in the community and greater hardship for many tenants.

"There are plenty of empty lots with no one living on them," Mrs. White replied. (According to a recent survey conducted by Mrs. Dunlap, there were 346 empty lots in East Garfield Park, and that was *before* the riot.)

"But would it be a good pattern for the community to follow?" Tony Henry asked. "Maybe if we're talking about single-family houses, we should think about building in the suburbs."

Mrs. White said that she would just as soon move to the suburbs. Mrs. Dunlap said that she preferred to remain in the city. Both agreed that no matter what kind of housing was built, it should be built for "poor people," and not for the "black middle class," and that the plan should include a safe, grassy area for children to play in.

Daniel Epstein said that with the legislation already on the books, it ought to be possible to build decent, low-cost accommodations for everyone (perhaps even in the suburbs, although land values were bound to be higher there). One provision of the 1968 Housing Law, for instance—title 235—provided for forty-year mortgages, with payments in some cases as low as *one percent a year.*

"If we do put together a whole block, can we get the money?" Mrs. White asked. "I mean, it ain't gonna be fifteen or twenty years?"

"It takes about a year to get your application through the paper shuffle at the Federal Housing Authority," Epstein said. "That's true no matter who you are—even Mayor Daley. Then it would take another few months for rehabilitation, or about a year for new construction. But the trouble is, even with the laws on the books, we don't know how much money there will be. The last couple of years, housing appropriations have been down to a trickle, because of the war."

It was finally decided to take a poll of the entire membership of the Tenants Union—which at that time numbered some five hundred families in sixty buildings—to find out what type of housing the people would like to live in if they had a choice.

"Things can be done if we get the people together," Tony Henry said by way of encouragement.

"The big thing," one of the lawyers commented, "is to let the community do its own planning."

Tony Henry is a large, solidly built man in his early thirties with a dark, squarish face and a dark, squarish beard. His physical appearance commands attention, especially when he wears a brightly colored African dashiki, but his surprisingly soft voice holds an audience even more effectively. As an adept in the relatively new field of community organization, he is painfully familiar with the kinds of problems that arise at meetings like the one at Our Lady of Sorrows Parish Hall—the difficulty of finding out what people really want in a community that has never heard the sound of its own voice, the enormous burdens placed on inexperienced local leaders who must guide others before their own on-the-job training is completed, the agony of trying to communicate across chasms of language, history, and culture with an outside world that offers a confusing mix of assistance and resistance; and the inevitable disappointments and pitifully slow pace of progress.*

---

* The Tenants Union eventually decided that the rehabilitation project at West Madison and Albany did not justify the investment of even a small portion of its available resources.

Although he is not a Quaker, Tony has evolved a personal philosophy of social change which he believes is quite close to the Quaker tradition, and which he sums up in the phrase: "You move when the people are ready to move." He first came into contact with the Service Committee in 1958, while studying at the University of Texas in Austin; during a sit-in campaign to integrate the local lunch counters, he and some friends organized a workshop in nonviolent tactics with the help of two representatives from the A.F.S.C. southwestern regional office. Later, after getting a master's degree in group work and community organizing from Springfield College, he went to Tanzania under the auspices of Voluntary International Service Assignments, an A.F.S.C. program that provided the organizational model for the Peace Corps. After a two-year tour, he came back to the United States and joined the staff of the East Garfield Park Project House. His first project there brought together groups of young children from the inner city and the Chicago area suburbs, in an imaginative round of activities aimed at breaking down the cultural isolation of both groups. Looking back, Tony is still convinced that this was a "good and valid program," which helped children of all races develop a better understanding of themselves and of the world they were growing up in. In the years since then, his interest has gradually shifted from promoting interracial communication to encouraging self-awareness and self-determination within minority groups. Yet he is still committed to nonviolent tactics as the best method to achieve his goals. And his view of the Service Committee has not changed: "There isn't another organization I know of that I would rather work for," he says, giving as his reason the Committee's ability to keep up with the times without losing its administrative grip, its courage, or its principles.

Like any other white liberal institution with a strong civil rights bent, the American Friends Service Committee has had its difficulties in adjusting to the rapidly changing priorities in the black ghetto during the past decade. Discouraged by the obduracy of a strongly racist establishment and rebuffed by the very people they were seeking to "integrate," many formerly staunch supporters have proclaimed the bankruptcy of the liberal ideas behind the civil rights movement—and have either withdrawn from the struggle in despair, or become radicalized, in the current sense of learning to accept the necessity of a violent solution for social inequities. But the Service Committee's memory is longer than that of most "movement" groups. Even before its early involvement in the battles against racial discrimination, Committee staff had been hard at work in American Indian communities, where one of the primary concerns was to preserve (or, in some cases, recreate) a sense of tribal identity in the face of encroachments by the dominant white culture. It was only natural then for the Service Committee to try to interpret the new cry of "Black Power" in light of this traditional concern.

The earliest Quakers used to speak of being compelled to take a certain action in order to remain "consistent" with their principles. Although they had rejected the notion of formal creeds and catechisms, they could easily reel off the list of evils they were against: intolerance, hypocrisy, injustice, violence, the exploitation of man by man. The job of putting together a detailed code of behavior they left to each man's conscience, as tempered by adverse circumstances, the world in general, and other people. This approach to the problem of day-to-day morality seems to contain the essence of true liberalism—as well as the kernel of the modern scientific method, which also assumes that fundamental consistencies can be discovered if one keeps testing likely hypotheses against a constantly changing reality. The trouble with such a method is that it demands so much hard work. Without constant vigilance, human reactions tend to become habitual, ossified, lifeless. In an effort to remain consistent

84

with its principles, the American Friends Service Committee has repeatedly sought to find common ground with new forces in our rapidly changing society. The strain has sometimes shaken the Committee to its roots—ideologically and administratively —but it has managed to survive with its most important programs and principles intact.

The A.F.S.C. was founded in Philadelphia in the spring of 1917 to provide a channel of alternative service for young Quakers who objected to the draft as a matter of conscience. More than five hundred conscientious objectors eventually went overseas under Service Committee auspices, to join a group of British Friends who had been working in hospitals, driving ambulances, and organizing relief projects among French civilians since the beginning of the War to End All Wars. When the Armistice was signed, the British and American C.O.'s stayed on to distribute food and clothing, and to help rebuild the shattered farms and villages. From the first, the A.F.S.C. mission tried to put into practice the Quaker belief that there is "that of God" in every man: There may be evil acts and evil institutions, but there are no irredeemably evil men. At one point the Service Committee was involved simultaneously in trying to heal the wounds of war in France, and in feeding one million starving children in Germany. The latter project aroused bitter opposition in some quarters, where the enemy was still considered the enemy even if he was under ten years of age and the fighting had ended.

The burden of humanitarian service proved harder to lay down than to take up. What had begun as a temporary wartime effort turned into an on-going commitment. During the next few years, A.F.S.C. representatives looked into the faces of the hungry and sick and dispossessed in Poland, Austria, Serbia, Syria, Bulgaria, Albania, China, Russia, and the coal-mining counties of Maryland, Kentucky, Tennessee, West Virginia, and Pennsylvania. By the end of the decade known as the Roaring Twenties, they had become acknowledged experts in the art of salvaging something human from the wreckage of man-made disasters—not fires, storms, and earthquakes but wars, depressions, repressions, riots and revolutions. There has hardly been a year in its history when the Service Committee has not been engaged in a large-scale relief mission somewhere in the United States or abroad. (In 1947, the A.F.S.C. and its English counterpart, the Friends Service Council of London, shared a Nobel Peace Prize for this work.) Indeed, the Committee is so firmly associated in the public mind with such missions that its efforts to bring about more basic social changes—to try to avoid the disasters—have often gone unnoticed. Without stinting on its emergency relief operations, the Committee has gradually evolved into a unique channel for what might be called "conscientious affirmation."

Among the principles affirmed by the people who work for the A.F.S.C. is the fundamental Quaker notion that there is no necessary conflict between idealism and practicality. The staff includes idealists, visionaries, mystics even, who take great pride in their sound business sense and efficient program management. In the fiscal year 1969, the Committee spent $7,002,041 around the world, and employed some 600 people (only one-third of whom were professing Quakers). Everyone connected with the Committee is constantly tinkering with its internal structure, searching (like administrators of all large institutions) for a better mix of individual initiative and corporate responsibility, as well as a better return on time and money invested.° At

---

° The Quaker reputation for mercantile shrewdness may be a little out of date, but it was staunchly upheld by the first A.F.S.C. mission to France after World War I. Faced with the task of restocking the battered economy of the Verdun region, Quaker volunteers discovered five enormous dumps

present, the work is administered through five Program Divisions—International Service, International Affairs, Youth Affairs, Peace Education and Community Relations—with national headquarters in Philadelphia, and ten regional offices. For the last ten years the Philadelphia office has been located at the corner of North Fifteenth and Race Streets, in a hundred-year old compound of grimy red-brick buildings which also houses the offices of the Philadelphia Yearly Meeting of the Religious Society of Friends, the Friends General Conference, the Friends Journal, and a number of other Quaker organizations. The decor of the A.F.S.C. building—which was formerly a Friends school —may be charitably described as "devoutly drab." (Quakers have always tended to be suspicious of the decorative arts; the traditional meeting houses are absolutely unadorned, without icons, stained glass, or even a simple cross.) The atmosphere inside is subdued but pleasantly informal. One of the last vestiges of the traditional "plain speech" to survive in current Quaker usage is the avoidance of superfluous titles, like Mr., Mrs., and Miss—at least when talking to other Quakers. When Committee members want to be really formal, they refer to a colleague by his given and Christian names; otherwise, everyone is on a first-name basis, from part-time secretaries on up to the Chairman of the Board.

Ultimate responsibility for Committee affairs rests with the members of a Corporation and a Board of Directors, all of whom are Quakers and receive no pay for their services. Overall administration is the province of an Executive Secretary (also a Quaker), who receives a salary and reports to the Board. At

of army surplus tools and equipment that the U.S. War Department was only too happy to part with for $50,000. The materiél was passed along to French farmers and businessmen at bargain prices, but even so, when the operation was completed, the A.F.S.C. "Dumps Department" showed a profit of $120,000—which was used to rebuild a bombed-out maternity hospital in the town of Chalons.

almost every administrative level, a distinction is maintained between paid professional staff, who operate specific projects, and unpaid, nonprofessional members of program committees, who theoretically set the guidelines and "employ" the staff. Each staff person is responsible to at least one program committee as well as to his administrative superiors. (Many, but not all, members of program committees are Quakers.) A particular project, such as the A.F.S.C. involvement with the East Garfield Park Tenants Union, may require at various times the scrutiny of the regional Executive Committee and the regional Executive Secretary, the Executive Committee and the Secretary of the Community Relations Division in Philadelphia, staff coordinators and special program committees from both the regional and the national office, the finance committees and finance secretaries at both levels and the national Executive Secretary and Board of Directors. The overlapping lines of communication look prohibitively complicated on paper, but the idea is to spread the responsibility for all decisions as widely as possible through the organization without engendering total stasis. When the system works, the Committee resembles a web of interlocking nerve centers, sensitive enough so that a ripple of activity in one corner soon sets the entire network trembling. The key to this sensitivity is a long-standing Quaker tradition of arriving at important decisions through a process of "consensus."

The term "Quaker" itself was originally a pejorative nickname, applied to members of the new religious sect in the midseventeenth century because they were supposed to "quake" in the presence of the Lord. The Quakers defiantly adopted the name (often referring to themselves in early literature as "the people called Quakers"), but they also coined for their movement the more euphonious epithets, "Children of the Light" and "First Publishers of the Truth." The Quakers held that God was made manifest to all men through an Inner Light, which could inform the faculties of reason and emotion, and point the way to true belief and correct behavior. By experience, they found that a group of dedicated men could reach agreement on a course of action if each member of the group laid himself open to the promptings of the Inner Light and at the same time listened sympathetically to his fellows, who, presumably, were being prompted by the same Light. The group experience was supposed to guide and temper individual insight; no man could ever be sure that *his* understanding of God's will was complete and sufficient. But by the same token, no man could be expected to act against his own conscience if he sincerely believed that he had been vouchsafed a piece of the Truth. As a result, although Quakers have been active in the struggle for many of the freedoms that are considered essential to a political democracy, they have avoided all forms of balloting in the conduct of their own business. Rather than force a question to a vote, which might freeze a minority in permanent opposition to the majority, the Quakers prefer to continue the discussion until everyone present feels comfortable with the "sense of the meeting" as articulated by the presiding clerk.

The discussion proceeds freely—everyone speaks out when he wishes, without having to be recognized by the chair—until the clerk says something like, "Friends, aren't we at the point now of very clear judgment on this matter?" If no one objects to his brief summary of that judgment, it is recorded in the minutes as an expression of the will of the entire assembly. On the other hand, if it becomes clear in the course of the discussion that there is no unity whatever on the subject, the clerk may say something like, "I get two strains of thought on this," or "Some Friends have expressed serious reservations about going ahead." After summarizing what seem to be the conflicting opinions, he may suggest referring the matter back to a smaller committee for further clarification. Again, if no one objects, the suggestion is considered to be "carried."

Theoretically, if just one member out of a meeting of one thousand feels that his conscience will not allow him to unite with the other nine hundred and ninety-nine on a certain decision, the nine hundred and ninety-nine will wait until the lone dissenter can be reconciled to their view, or until a compromise embodying his objection can be worked out. In practice, a Quaker consensus does not mean that every participant enthusiastically supports the proposed action, but it does mean that everyone with reservations has been given full opportunity to make his views known, and, if these go unheeded by the majority, has voluntarily agreed to "stand aside" and let the others proceed. It is understood that once a consensus has been reached in this manner, the responsibility for the recorded decision falls equally on *all* participants.

To function at all, such a process requires a presiding clerk who is alert to every nuance of the discussion, a high degree of what the Quakers call "likemindedness," and a great deal of humility all around. (Members of the majority have consciences too; the Quaker Meetings in colonial Pennsylvania finally disowned—that is, refused to sit in fellowship with—the small minority of members who, after several years of Friendly persuasion, would not free their slaves.) The Quaker approach to decision-making may break down entirely when opinion is so evenly divided on matters of conscience that neither side can feel comfortable with a compromise. (This is what happened during the doctrinal schisms that rent the Religious Society of Friends in the United States during the nineteenth century.) Even at best, the consensus process is time-consuming and exhausting, and it would seem to be a heavy cross to bear for a religious congregation, much less for a far-flung corporate enterprise like the Service Committee. But for the people directly involved—Quakers and non-Quakers—it has often proved to be a most reliable arbiter in the day-to-day business of allocating limited resources according to the dictates of conscience and the demands of efficiency.

One of the people involved in this incredibly complicated and often heartbreaking business is Kale Williams, the executive secretary of the Chicago Regional Office of the A.F.S.C. In the winter of 1968, Kale took an eighteen-month leave of absence from his Chicago post to direct a Quaker relief program in Nigeria. This kind of occupational leap is not uncommon among Committee staff members, even for those who, like Kale, are married and have three children. At the age of forty-four, Kale had already headed the Chicago office for ten years, an unusually long tenure for an executive secretary. During that decade, he had seen the local emphasis in program shift from racial integration to community organization; he had seen the mood of young draft-refusers shift from conscientious objection to open resistance; and he had witnessed the rise and fall of nonviolence as a "popular" tactic in the struggle for social change. He himself had marched through the streets of Chicago with Martin Luther King, Jr., taken a brick in the head, gone to jail, defended the radicalism of the Committee to conservative-minded contributors and the conservatism of the Committee to young radicals, and tried to keep up with new developments without violating his own convictions, which were largely formed by a wartime experience before he was twenty years old.

He was born in Cedar Vale, Kansas, a small town of 850, where his father sold automobiles and farm equipment. His family was nominally Methodist, and he attended the local church and Sunday school as a matter of course. By his own admission, he was a serious young man with an "idealistic" bent, and when he graduated from high school in the spring of 1943, he volunteered with great enthusiasm to help defend Freedom and Democracy as a radar technician in the United States Navy. Assigned to a light cruiser operating in the Pacific, he saw action off the Philippines, off Okinawa, and eventually off the coast of Japan itself. When it was all over, and the forces of Freedom and Democracy had triumphed, he decided that he would never again be able to take part in organized killing.

Thinking about that decision many years later, Kale recalled that it had not come "all in one flash. It was more of a gradual process of disillusionment with what I saw around me. Part of it was my first encounter with racial discrimination; I don't think I'd ever seen a Negro at home, but I had been taught that discrimination was bad, and I was naïve enough to be upset at the caste system in the Navy. All the Negroes on shipboard were messboys, except during battle when they were invariably given the least desirable and most dangerous task, as ammunition handlers below decks, putting shells on elevators.

"Then there was an American atrocity I witnessed. . . . We had hit some Japanese planes in one battle, and their pilots parachuted out over the task force. As a radar technician, I wore earphones that were tuned into the gunnery circuits, and I could hear the chief gunnery officer break into a paroxysm of rage and obscenity while the 20- and 40-millimeter guns fired on the helpless parachutists. I *knew* some of those gunners, and I knew they were perfectly decent men, and somehow I began to get the idea that the real problem was not the Japanese but war itself, as an institution that could turn otherwise decent men to this. When Hiroshima came, it only seemed like the supreme illustration of the callousness of war as an institution. I had talked to American pilots who had flown over Japan without seeing any sign of resistance; they all felt that Japan was already defeated. And then, after the Bomb, after the surrender, to go ashore in Japan and to see life going on . . . to see human beings, some friendly, some not, trying to raise children and gather food . . . you looked around and you thought, This is the enemy?"

After receiving his discharge in 1946, Kale Williams took advantage of the G.I. Bill to study social science at the University of Chicago, with the idea of becoming a high school teacher. Living in a dormitory with other veterans, he began to work out his personal pacifist position in arguments with fellow students. "One of my friends said that I sounded like a couple he knew. He introduced us, and they turned out to be Quakers. It was the first time I realized there might be other people who had an organized body of concepts like mine." The Quaker couple were active in a summer work-camp program for young people that the A.F.S.C. sponsored; Kale served as a volunteer for several years, and in 1951 he interrupted his progress toward a master's degree in social science to fill a temporary staff vacancy in the Committee's Chicago office.

Nineteen fifty-one was the year that the Service Committee took part in an abortive campaign to breach the residential color line in the Chicago suburb of Cicero. White residents reacted massively and violently to the prospect of Negro neighbors; and the civil rights advocates withdrew from the field when it became clear that the lives of the pioneering black families were in danger. But the Service Committee refused to consider the defeat as anything but temporary.

Immediately after the war, Committee personnel had been instrumental in starting a merit-employment drive in Chicago's department stores and banks, which, after a slow start, had brought about a noticeable change in hiring policies. Now the Committee decided to establish an ambitious Housing Opportunities Program, to work with white and black families who were interested in creating a genuinely open housing market throughout the metropolitan area.

ON DOING GOOD

In 1955, the Committee purchased a building on West Jackson Street, to use as a base for youth-service projects in the area known as East Garfield Park. "We chose East Garfield," Kale explained, "because we thought it was typical of the problems of the city at the time. It was a neighborhood in transition, still mostly Italian and Irish, but with an increasing percentage of Negroes, and we hoped to stabilize it as an integrated community. Our first experience in the area was to be under physical attack. When we moved in, the house was still several blocks ahead of the Negro line; and there we were, with black faces going in and out of the front door. . . . Bricks were thrown and at least one shot was fired. Of course, from what we know now, it seems naïve in the extreme for us to have thought that putting in ten or twelve youth-service volunteers would have any effect on a population shift of that dimension." Statistics show the black ghetto in Chicago has been expanding over the last two decades at a steady rate of between two and three blocks per week. With the exception of a few hundred Negro families that groups like the A.F.S.C. have helped to place in the suburbs, black expansion in Metropolitan Chicago has been channeled into certain clearly defined corridors within the core city.

The Negroes' block-by-block "advance" through certain deteriorating residential neighborhoods is, of course, a direct function of the segregated housing market. The Negro community of Chicago is both a slum—because most of its housing is substandard and getting worse—and a ghetto, because its inhabitants cannot choose to live elsewhere. In recent years, according to an estimate made by a staff member of the A.F.S.C. regional office, less than *one percent* of all properties listed for sale in realtors' offices in the Chicago metropolitan area have been "available" to Negro buyers, and these properties were almost invariably contiguous to the existing ghetto.

The humiliations and frustrations that qualified Negroes are subjected to in the suburban housing market throughout the country were documented in appalling detail in a report compiled by the A.F.S.C. in 1967. Five years after President Kennedy had ordered an end to any form of discrimination in all federally owned or aided housing, the Service Committee found that Executive Order 11063 was "being widely and flagrantly violated by builders, brokers and lenders." Furthermore, "implementation of the Order by the Federal Housing Administration and the Veterans Administration has been at least ineffective, and at worst subversive of the goal of equal opportunity in housing. Even our experience in the frustrations of community relations work," the report continued, "did not fully prepare A.F.S.C. staff workers for the webs of obfuscation that have been encountered by them and by the homeseekers with whom they have worked in attempts to secure housing covered by the Executive Order." *

Aside from the other hardships it imposes, the severely restricted housing market for Negroes is responsible for one of the cruelest ironies of the entire racial situation in the North: Although blacks lag far behind whites in almost every recognized index of living standards, the category in which the two groups are the closest to equality is the monthly rent bill. In 1966, Chicago's Negro families, which were one-fifth larger than their white counterparts, lived in dwellings that were one-fifth smaller and five times as dilapidated—yet they paid the *same* median rent, and they paid it out of incomes that were only two-thirds as large. (A Negro college graduate in Chicago earns less than a white high school dropout.) To put it another way, white fami-

* The thirteen Kafkaesque case histories appended to the report make instructive reading for any white liberal who wonders why so many black Americans have turned their backs on the dream of Integration Now.

lies, who have more money, spend no more for their superior housing than black people do for their slums—a state of affairs that sociologists refer to as a "color tax."

Given all these figures, it can be seen just how naïve the Service Committee was in 1955 to think that the actions of a few well-meaning individuals, a handful of youthful idealists, could halt such a social juggernaut in its tracks. But it would be naïveté of another sort to assume that individuals can *never* have an impact in such matters. While it is no doubt true that the drive toward residential segregation in Chicago was the product of vast, anonymous socio-economic forces, there is evidence that the pace and timing of the drive were at least partly determined by a small group of powerful men intent on carrying out an explicitly racist policy.

In 1917 the Chicago Real Estate Board, which has the power to license realtors, appointed a special Committee on Negro Housing "to investigate and deal with the colored people problem." The problem, as seen by the realtors, was what to do with the increasing numbers of Negroes who were flocking to Chicago (mainly from rural areas in the South) to find work in the city's booming wartime industries. The solution, as drafted by the Committee on Negro Housing, was to discontinue, "in the interest of all," the then common practice of selling single houses to colored families in predominantly white areas. Instead, the Negro population was to be consolidated in a few homogeneous areas, and the future expansion of such areas was to be on a contiguous, block-by-block basis. This recommendation was buttressed by the argument—which was in question even then and has since been disproved in a significant number of cases—that property values *invariably* plummet "the moment the first colored family moves into a block." The Chicago Real Estate Board began urging property owners in white neighborhoods to sign race-restrictive covenants, which stipulated that the owners would not sell, rent, lease, or convey property to members of minority groups. Such covenants were considered legally binding if a certain percentage of owners in a given neighborhood agreed to sign. Outside the *newly drawn* ghetto lines, individual blocks were apparently earmarked for reclamation from earlier Negro encroachment; in 1920 the Chicago Board sent its "felicitations" to one "neighborhood improvement organization" that announced it had prevented the move-ins of fifty-seven Negro families in the Hyde Park–Kenwood district. (There had been twenty-four fire bombings of Negro homes in Chicago in the previous two years; most of them had occurred in the Hyde Park–Kenwood district.) To make the point even clearer, the Chicago Board voted to expel any member who sold or rented to a Negro in an all-white neighborhood.

Chicago seems to have been a pace-setter in this field. In 1924 the National Association of Real Estate Boards adopted a similar provision in its code of ethics, threatening violators with loss of the privileges of the title "Realtor." And in 1938 the Federal Housing Authority declared in its underwriting manual that "If a neighborhood is to retain stability, it is necessary that properties continue to be occupied by the same social and racial group." The F.H.A. specifically recommended the use of restrictive covenants to keep out "inharmonious racial groups" and even included a "model covenant" in its manual.°

° The ostensible reasons for these actions was to discourage "block-busting." A block-buster is a real estate agent who places a black family in an all-white block with the express purpose of scaring the white residents into selling to him, usually at far below market prices, property which he can then resell to incoming black families at considerably above market prices. Block-busting has been generally deplored by both blacks and whites, but the difference between the block-busters' tactics and the operation of an open housing market ought to be clear enough to anyone who examines the matter. The profits of the block-buster are derived from the panic of the white residents, and he tries to play on their fears with whispering

ON DOING GOOD

The United States Supreme Court ruled in 1948 that neighborhood race-restrictive covenants were unenforceable in the courts. But by then the momentum of residential segregation in cities like Chicago was probably too strong to be reversed, even if the ensuing civil-rights legislation had been firmly enforced by federal, state and local governments, and consistently supported by a majority of the white liberal community.

Although the effort of the American Friends Service Committee to influence the racial makeup of East Garfield Park was clearly a failure, it did at least provide a ready-made base for participation in the next phase of civil-rights agitation—helping the ghetto organize itself. On almost every index of poverty—mean level of income, number of families receiving Aid to Dependent Children, incidence of tuberculosis, infant mortality rate—East Garfield Park ranked among the five lowest of Chicago's seventy-five recognized community districts. It had no large industry, and unlike some slum areas, it did not even have one highly visible institution—a famous university or a major hospital—to pin some of its troubles on and give it a power lever in urban politics. (Large public or philanthropic institutions can be terrible bullies, but they can also be bullied in return, in a way that anonymous slumlords cannot.) As a result, despite all its documented need, East Garfield Park had remained at the lowest end of the scale in the quality and quantity of outside assistance.

Many of the basic principles of what is now known as community organization were first laid down by Saul Alinsky, the self-styled "professional radical," whose Industrial Areas Foundation has been training community leaders in Chicago since

campaigns, misleading statistics, unsigned circulars filled with dire warnings about the future of the area, and so on. Far from combating such tactics the F.H.A. and Chicago Real Estate Board actually abetted them, by stamping their imprimatur on the "evidence" which the block-busters so often cited.

1941. "Alinsky was ahead of most people in understanding the forces that shape urban areas," Kale Williams said. "But we reject his approach of using *any* kind of conflict to create a situation in which the group that's out of power can gain power." Alinsky, who was also ahead of most people in identifying the Well-Meaning Liberal as the arch-enemy of the poor and oppressed—has defined American society as a brutal competition among a wide variety of economic and political blocs; he sees his task as welding the formerly impotent into a new bloc strong enough to grab a piece of the action. "In one of the Chicago communities organized by Alinsky-trained people," Kale went on, "the method used was to identify the enemy specifically as the 'Jewish landlords.' We faced a similar situation in East Garfield Park with the Tenants Union. But our appeal was different. We started off by saying that we'd respect the humanity of the landlords but that nothing would keep us from telling the truth about conditions, and naming the individuals that we felt were responsible."

The use of a scapegoat to rouse an apathetic community is not only bad morals, in the view of Friends like Kale, but also bad tactics. "What we're striving to discover is a method of organizing people in a neighborhood to deal with their own problems so that the neighborhood remains in touch with the wider community. That's absolutely necessary because so many of the resources are out there, not in the ghetto." (In a number of cases in Chicago, a community group has purchased a rundown building from an outside landlord, only to discover that there was no way under prevailing conditions to maintain a decent building at rents that the tenants could afford.)

The art of encouraging community organization in ghetto areas can be frustrating to social reformers (of whatever ideological bent) who think in terms of grand strategies and strict timetables. Nothing is more suspect in the ghetto than great ambition. The more ambitious a community organization is at the outset—the more problems it tries to tackle and the more promises it makes—the more likely it is to disintegrate within a few months, leaving nothing behind but a heightened sense of deprivation among local residents. The neighborhood groups that survive, according to Kale, are those that spring up in response to one small, tangible, immediate, and emotionally charged issue—and build from there. The first stages, especially, are booby-trapped with what seem to be unresolvable paradoxes. If the indigenous group is to avoid a damaging client-patron relation with the outsiders who offer help, there must be strong local leaders. But the pool of potential leaders in a ghetto community is, in Kale's words, "tragically thin. A middle-class group in Hyde Park can get competent, nearly full-time staff work from volunteers—housewives, retired people, businessmen—but you can't do this in a place like East Garfield Park. No one with the kind of skills you need has the time to give them free."

The obvious alternative is to train and pay local people, which takes time and money and a great deal of tact. The time required is bound to conflict with the urgency of whatever crisis brought the organization into existence in the first place, and the need for outside funds conflicts with the desire for self-determination that motivates the best of the new leaders. "There is a kind of natural life-cycle to any community effort," Kale said. "In the beginning, when you form around a specific issue, there's a high degree of enthusiasm and participation; then there's a natural attrition as people become disillusioned by the slow progress and lack of rewards. That's the make or break time with community organizations: if they don't move very quickly toward real independence, it gets harder and harder to make them viable." Yet conditions in the ghetto being what they are, the need for financial assistance will continue long past this point. The only way out of the paradox is to find a source of outside funds with virtually no strings attached—a role that not even the American Friends Service Committee relishes.

One of Tony Henry's former colleagues at the Quaker Project House in East Garfield Park described the task of a community organizer as essentially that of an "issue-fisher." In a community where everyday conditions are so grim that apathy may be considered a survival trait, it takes an especially horrible incident to qualify as an "issue." In the summer of 1965, a woman whose daughter had died after eating lead-based paint from a piece of fallen plaster in her home came to Project House to ask if something couldn't be done to save other neighborhood children from the same fate. (The effects of lead-poisoning are cumulative and even when not fatal, the ingestion of lead-based paint can cause paralysis, blindness and permanent brain damage.) With the aid of Project House staff, a Citizens' Committee to End Lead-Poisoning was formed, and the group petitioned the city health authorities to launch an intensive case-finding program to bring under control the so-called "silent epidemic," which had already taken the lives of more than fifteen children that year. The campaign, as ghetto campaigns go, was accounted a success: In 1966 the number of children's deaths traceable to lead-poisoning fell to six.

Meanwhile, the pace of community organization in East Garfield Park had been given a tremendous impetus by the decision of the Rev. Martin Luther King, Jr., and his Southern Christian Leadership Conference to begin an ambitious campaign of non-violent direct action against slum conditions (especially segregated housing) in Chicago. Project House was chosen as a field headquarters, and an umbrella group called the East Garfield Park Union to End Slums was put together, with representatives from twenty-seven local organizations on the steering committee. Dr. King's campaign in the spring and summer of 1966 was a dramatic test of the methods of the Southern-based civil-rights movement in a large Northern city; his followers marched through the streets, held prayer vigils in front of the offices of uncooperative real estate agents, picketed, and eventually conferred with business, labor, religious and political leaders to work out what came to be known as the Summit Agreement to end housing discrimination in Chicago.

The implementation of this Summit Agreement proved to be disappointing, and many people have identified the inconclusive Chicago campaign as the swan song of the civil-rights movement itself. But there were a number of smaller victories, among them the signing in July of the first collective bargaining agreement between organized tenants, represented by the Union to End Slums, and a Chicago landlord with extensive holdings in East Garfield Park. When the citywide drive faltered, the East Garfield Park Tenants Union emerged as a wholly indigenous group around a core of dedicated local leaders (with the guidance and financial backing of the A.F.S.C.).

Since then, the Union has undergone several changes of name, survived some hard times, and continued to grow. A contract with a second landlord was negotiated; but like the first, it proved difficult to enforce. The Union has engaged in almost perpetual rent strikes and rent-withholding actions, which occasionally result in repairs to dangerously decayed buildings, and which keep a battery of volunteer lawyers busy defending tenants against a succession of five-day eviction notices. When one city agency took steps to demolish some officially condemned buildings before another city agency had found adequate new housing for tenants, the Union staged sit-ins in Mayor Daley's offices; following the nonviolent but persistent demonstrations, the mayor's aides managed to find acceptable shelter for the families, and even displayed a new willingness to confer with tenants' representatives on rulings that directly affected their well-being. Lately, the emphasis has shifted away from negotiating new contracts with individual landlords toward establishing, through legal and political actions, certain basic rights common to all tenants.

Landlord-tenant relationships in the United States today are largely governed by provisions of Anglo-Saxon common law that go back, almost without change, to the Middle Ages. Under these provisions—which were originally designed to apply to the rental of *land*, not housing—the landlord's obligation ends when he makes his property available to the tenant for a stipulated time. Even if the property becomes uninhabitable during this time, the landlord need not lift a finger, except to collect the rent which the tenant must go on paying. In Chicago, the implications of this one-sided contract are spelled out in almost unreadably small print on a standard lease form that bears the imprimatur of the Chicago Real Estate Board. The landlord's obligations to the tenant are mentioned in a single sentence that refers to the maintenance of the "floor, interior and exterior walls, supports, ceiling and roof"—but this is followed by a disclaimer that begins: "The failure to keep any of the foregoing in repair shall not affect the obligation of TENANT to pay rent . . ." On the other hand, when a tenant signs the lease, he not only waives his right to sue the landlord for any reason whatsoever, but he also agrees to plead guilty to any complaint the landlord might bring against him in the future. (The lease actually authorizes the *landlord's* lawyer to plead guilty in the name of the *tenant* and at his expense, without even having to inform the tenant that legal proceedings have begun.)

It is true that Chicago, like most cities, is committed under its municipal code to see that private residential buildings are maintained in a livable condition; tenants do have the right to complain to the proper authorities about violations of community standards of safety and cleanliness. But until recently, the pressure on landlords to comply with the code was gravely undercut by the fact that tenants were legally bound to go on paying full rent even in buildings with long-standing, multiple violations. And if a tenant in such a building was receiving welfare money to help pay his rent—as nearly a third of the families in East Garfield Park were—the Cook County Department of Public Aid was put in the position of subsidizing the landlord's income on property that constituted a menace to the public welfare.

In addition, the city court system was so arranged that cases involving five-day eviction notices and cases involving code violations were heard in two separate jurisdictions—Eviction Court and Equity Court. The only issue in eviction proceedings was whether or not the tenant had paid his rent; the state of the premises was not admissible as a defense for nonpayment. As a result, a tenant could be evicted in one court while his landlord was being fined for a number of major violations—rat infestation, falling plaster, no heat, no electricity—in the other court. In cases of extreme negligence, the Equity Court judge could place a building in receivership; the receiver (usually an agency of the city) was supposed to renovate the building out of current revenue and then return it to its rightful owner. Unfortunately, by the time the legal maneuvers were completed, the property had often deteriorated to such an extent that it was no longer possible to bring it up to code standards within the budgetary limits set by statute. Instead of renovation, the outcome was often condemnation and demolition—one more empty lot along the decaying boulevards, and another group of families thrown into the already constricted housing market.

The new strength of tenants' organizations in Chicago spurred some important changes in these conditions. The Cook County Department of Public Aid began withholding rent-payment checks on behalf of welfare recipients living in substandard buildings. An Equity Court judge began reducing rents by as much as half in buildings where the city agency serving as receiver had failed to correct major code violations in a reasonable length of time. And for the first time, defendants in Eviction Court were granted the right to a jury trial.

Encouraged by the continued vitality of the Tenants Union—which now represented a thousand tenants in buildings throughout the city and had changed its name accordingly to the *Chicago* Tenants Union—Tony Henry decided to transfer his energies, with A.F.S.C. blessings, to organizing a nationwide movement of tenants-rights groups. Late in 1969, at a conference in St. Louis attended by delegates from a hundred local unions with an estimated membership of more than 50,000, the National Tenants Organization was formed. Jesse Gray, a rent-strike pioneer in New York City, was named chairman, and Tony became the full-time executive director. In releasing him to the new group, the Service Committee also released enough funds to underwrite the program until N.T.O. could apply for tax-exempt status and secure more permanent support elsewhere.

On the local level, tenants unions will no doubt continue to sit-in, and squat-in, and use other pressure tactics to redress specific grievances while demanding a larger voice in the day-to-day management of both public and privately-owned housing. The potential strength of the tenants-rights movement extends far beyond the ghetto; some of the most successful local groups have been organized in solidly white middle-class housing projects. Besides coordinating all these activities, the Washington office of N.T.O. will try to make its power felt in national policy-making circles. Tony himself sees little chance of improving low-income housing without substantial federal subsidies—as well as some sort of legislative package that does the same thing for tenants rights that New Deal legislation did for the rights of organized labor.

ON DOING GOOD

The role that the Service Committee played in the genesis of the National Tenants Organization is a perfect example of what is known as "program devolution" in A.F.S.C. jargon. Since its own resources are so limited, the Committee prefers to function as an experimenter and enabler in its community relations work, putting itself out of a job as soon as a program is strong enough to go its own way. Ultimately, the success of a particular venture in community organization depends on the strength of the local leaders who become involved in what Tony Henry calls a "kindergarten in power." In some ways, the lives of Mrs. White and Mrs. Dunlap and their associates in East Garfield Park have been changed greatly by their involvement with the Tenants Union, but the changes, like those in the community at large, only point up how much remains to be done.

Both Mrs. White and Mrs. Dunlap, for instance, became experts at thwarting eviction attempts, by legal or extralegal means. Mrs. White has described the process in these words: "I had a call about a girl who was on the street. The county welfare people were withholding her rent because her building was so bad, but a bailiff came anyway and set her things right out in the street. We went over and got the whole block together and moved her back in. Then a policeman came—he *said* he was a policeman—and he said he had a warrant to move her out again, but I looked at it and it was only a piece of paper about a code violation. I called up the county and they said to ignore it. So that girl stayed put. . . . Every time a tenant gets an eviction notice, we go to court with him; if we don't, and he goes by himself, he's just out!"

The building in which Mrs. White herself lived was one of the first to be covered by a Union contract and—when the tenants accused the landlord of violating the agreement—one of the first to go on rent strike. Although the tangible results of such ac-

tions are often hard to see, Mrs. White soon became a firm be-
liever in the power of rent strikes as an equalizer in confrontations between landlord and tenant. "I remember when my
landlord wouldn't even talk to us," she said. "Now he gives us
the best of respect. He's a very strange man. I can't figure him
out and he can't figure me out. In court we'll get up and fight
each other, and then he drives me home afterwards and tells me
how much he's doing for black people. He keeps saying it's all
the government's fault. I really believe he's a nice person. He
has spent a lot of money in some buildings, and the kids come
in and just tear everything up. They take bottles and knock
holes in the wall. The kids in *our* building, the parents got them
controlled; but it's the others down the block—every age from
thirteen on down to two. . . . The Union has tried to do something about it, but you can't talk to other people's children.
That's why we need play lots, to give them a chance to play."

Mrs. White spoke with almost maternal pride about the skill
and dedication of her brigade of volunteer lawyers. But her only
comment on the subject of integration was that "maybe it will
come back someday. For now, we got to do it for ourselves." She
cited the case of another landlord who fought the Union strenuously in court: "He can be very nice. He believes in begging
your pardon if he says anything wrong. But he's the one who
rented an apartment on West Madison for $105 a month—the
woman wasn't even in the Union but we went over to take a
look, and the whole roof was out; the rain came right in. We
asked the landlord what on earth did he rent that apartment for,
and he said he had a heart, and this woman needed a place to
stay after the riot. So we said, 'If you have a heart, why don't
you put a roof on?' . . . I tell you, skin don't make nobody—
some of the dirtiest people in the world are black—but I'd
rather for a black person to own my building even if he couldn't

afford to fix it up. I don't think it's right for a landlord to come in here and rent fifty or sixty buildings, and he lives out in Oak Park."

Many of the white absentee landlords active in real estate in East Garfield Park today built up their holdings in the previous, nonblack era, or inherited from relatives who did. Others, who more closely fit the stereotype of "slumlord," moved in as speculators to take advantage of the black community's lack of capital; the ability to get an ordinary bank mortgage is a mighty economic lever in an area like East Garfield. Some landlords—especially those in the first category—insist that owning slum property is a financial hardship, and claim that they would be glad to get out if they could only find a qualified buyer. The large number of structures simply abandoned by their owners would seem to substantiate this claim. But according to Kale Williams, the amount of profit that can be squeezed out of seemingly derelict ghetto buildings should never be underestimated. As just one example, Kale told of the experience of a regular contributor to the Committee, a Quaker businessman who managed commercial properties in Chicago. Based on his personal knowledge of commercial real estate, he had tended to dismiss the Committee's reports of profiteering in ghetto housing as the typical exaggerations of a "cause" organization. Then a client of his inherited some property that turned out to be largely slum dwellings, including a number in East Garfield Park. When the Quaker businessman had finished examining both the properties and the account books, he came to Kale to confess that he was shocked by what he had seen. In the hall of one of the buildings, he had stumbled over a dead rat; in the account books, he had discovered that an "inexcusably small percentage of gross income" had been assigned to maintenance and repairs over the years—despite the fact that the buildings were showing a fat profit.

After a long enough period of such calculated abuse, the land-lord who says that he cannot keep his property up to code standards on current rents may very well be telling the truth. Having bled the property dry, he stands to reap an extra divi-dend if he can sell out—under federally assured terms—to an inexperienced community organization that plunges into a reha-bilitation project without expert advice. Even with all the gov-ernment programs available, Kale said, there is probably noth-ing that can be done with many of the buildings except to demolish them, "unless the slumlords themselves put some of their ill-gotten profits back into the houses and rehabilitate them, and from then on agree to accept a normal return."

Even to suggest such an alternative—getting the bad guys to rectify their past sins at their own expense—may sound typi-cally impractical and Quakerish. But in fact, one successful model for such a program already exists, in Chicago's Operation Breadbasket, the economic arm of the Southern Christian Lead-ership Conference. Under the leadership of Jesse Jackson, a former lieutenant of Dr. King, Operation Breadbasket has been using "moral pressures" on white businessmen who want to keep doing business in the ghetto; the idea is to get them first to admit to previous discriminatory practices, and then to guaran-tee in writing that they will change their ways in such specific matters as hiring more Negroes, banking at Negro banks, adver-tising in ghetto newspapers, and letting contracts to Negro con-cessionaires. The prime targets have been large chain stores with numerous outlets in the ghetto; tactics have included direct appeals to conscience, informational picketing, adverse publicity in the news media and the threat of consumers' boycotts.

The American Friends Service Committee and the Southern Christian Leadership Conference have often influenced one an-other. They have borrowed each other's ideas, exchanged staff personnel, and worked together in a number of ambitious programs, including the Poor People's Campaign, to provoke major social changes through nonviolent means. (The Service Committee has usually played the role of "silent partner," which is the way both organizations prefer it.) In general, the two groups share not only the same goals but also the same insight into the relation between goals and means. While neither would subscribe to Saul Alinsky's avowed policy of "rubbing raw the festering sores of social discontent," both the S.C.L.C. and the A.F.S.C. accept the necessity of shaking the *status quo*, perhaps to its foundation, to bring about a more just society. Indeed, the Service Committee's penchant for taking sides in domestic strife has often confused friends (and exasperated critics) who think of the Quakers first of all as peacemakers. The credibility of the Quakers' antiwar testimony has always rested on their refusal to take sides in any armed conflict (even when their own country was involved). Yet the whole thrust of the Service Committee's domestic programs has been a public advocacy of the physically powerless, the economically distressed, the racially and religiously persecuted. There are some Quakers who would prefer to see the A.F.S.C. assume the role of honest broker domestically as well as internationally; who think that the Committee would do better to try to heal old wounds rather than take part in new (even if nonviolent) confrontations. "We had a real go-round on this in the Committee about ten years ago," Kale Williams said. "The more involved we became in community race relations the more we had to face the fact that our workers were at least temporarily *increasing* tensions in a community. Was this Quaker reconciliation? Eventually, the Board of Directors adopted a minute which said that true reconciliation means more than just two people in a conflict being reconciled to each other —both must be reconciled to a common concept of justice."

Even with this redefinition, no one on the Service Committee has any illusions about the ease of trying to combine the roles of advocate and reconciler. It is taken for granted that the key to success lies in a strict adherence to the principles of nonviolence, since only a nonviolent challenge to power and privilege leaves the door open to a recognition that both sides have a stake in building a more just society. The trouble is, everyone in the Committee has his own idea of what constitutes nonviolence, and very few are satisfied with their own formulations, much less with anyone else's.

Kale Williams' personal guidelines to nonviolent advocacy were formed during his ten years' experience in Chicago, where the interplay between the forces of change and repression has been unusually instructive. Two examples come most vividly to mind: The summer of 1966, when the Chicago police resorted to violence to protect the open-housing advocates who marched behind Martin Luther King; and the summer of 1968, when the Chicago police resorted to violence to disperse the anti-Vietnam War demonstrators during the Democratic convention.

In 1966, Dr. King led his followers through hostile white neighborhoods in order to make a witness at the offices of real estate agents who played an important role in maintaining the segregated housing market in the city. Mayor Daley deplored the demonstrations but ordered police protection for the marchers. In almost every way, the marchers' behavior was exemplary: they sang spirituals, they did not retaliate when rocks were hurled at them, they kept proclaiming that their actions were motivated by love for all men—including the white rock-throwers, and Mayor Daley. Despite the physical dangers they faced, the demonstrators remained orderly and unflinching. Yet the ambitious campaign, in Kale's words, "failed to generate any greater spiritual power" once the police protection became so efficient that it "effectively protected the marchers and inflicted violence and suffering upon the antagonists." (On several occasions, the police drove off white hecklers with nightsticks and even threatened them with drawn revolvers.) The immediate purpose of nonviolent protest is to bring about a change in conditions without the use of force on either side; however, if violence *does* occur, it is assumed that the blows will be directed against the demonstrators themselves who are (or should be) fully prepared for the risks involved. Once a course of action begins producing victims among the general populace—whether or not they are "innocent" bystanders—then such actions, by Kale's guidelines, can no longer be considered truly nonviolent. Unable to devise an alternative strategy in the time available, the leaders of the open-housing campaign could only continue with the marches, while tensions in the city mounted, positions hardened, and prospects for meaningful reconciliation receded. Rather than a failure of nonviolence *per se*, Kale sees the outcome as a failure of imagination on the part of the nonviolent leaders (including himself).

The police violence during the Democratic convention in 1968 was primarily directed at the antiwar demonstrators—as anyone in the nation with a television set could plainly see. But from Kale's point of view, too many people in the streets had been trying to exploit an already explosive situation, and were therefore at least partly to blame for the blow-up. The National Mobilization Committee to End the War in Vietnam, which coordinated the major demonstrations, was a diffuse *ad hoc* group, and there was wide disagreement among its leaders concerning the means and ends of the protest. The A.F.S.C. was not an official sponsor of the Mobilization, but it did lend office space to the group, and several A.F.S.C. staff members became associated with specific activities that seemed to have been conceived in a spirit of nonviolence. (Kale himself was among thirty-one persons who were arrested opposite the International Amphitheater during a nonviolent vigil to protest the suppression of human rights "in Vietnam, Czechoslovakia, American ghettos, and the streets of Chicago.")

In a report on the events of Convention Week, however, Kale wrote that "strategies of disruption and provocation which have been peripheral in other large demonstrations became a dominant strategy in this one." He was referring to the threatening tone of public announcements by certain spokesmen for the Mobilization, the use of degrading epithets against police and other public officials, the advocacy and use of "mobile tactics" designed to harass the police, the call for "any means possible" to get through police lines, and the "use and justification of weapons and missiles."

For Kale, the exchange of degrading epithets—"using the word 'pig' for people"—is an act of violence, even if no bricks or punches are thrown, whereas physical trespass on public or private property, or open disobedience of a legal statute, may be a genuinely nonviolent act if it is carried out under "a clear and explicitly nonviolent discipline." Ideally, this discipline would include the following items: the drafting and prior public announcement of practical, limited goals which do not make impossible demands on the "target population"; detailed contingency planning for each phase of the demonstration; full and uninterrupted communication about goals and tactics with everyone directly concerned—the participants, the authorities, the potential antagonists—and complete openness about the possible risks to every individual and the steps being taken to minimize them. In other words, an act of nonviolent advocacy or protest should be at least as carefully planned and executed as the most routine military operation or guerrilla foray.

"The phrase 'nonviolent direct action,'" Kale said, "is too often used to cover anything that isn't a physical attack on another person. But to take thousands of people who have been

113

marching around all day, tired and hungry, all fired up with speeches, and expect them to remain nonviolent—especially when they've had no training—in a confrontation that offers no constructive alternative to either side . . . That is *not* nonviolence as I define it."

Perhaps the most important ingredient in a truly nonviolent discipline, Kale added, is a willingness on the part of the demonstrators to "accept suffering and the legal penalties for their actions." This is so important because the ultimate goal of all nonviolent action is "to re-establish a real community, and law is one expression of such a community. People who seek to evade the penalties for disobeying a bad law assume a legitimacy for their actions—untested—that they would deny others. There's an element in the New Left that is trying to turn the issues into a contest for power. It might conceivably succeed, although the forces of repression would probably win, but it would not succeed in redressing the basic human problems. A person who believes as I do would probably have to oppose that kind of government." On similar grounds, he holds that such "symbolic" acts as burning draft cards and pouring blood on Selective Service records are "essentially reactionary—the real problem isn't the existence of the records; it's changing the minds of the majority of people who think that the draft laws are necessary."

His faith in the efficacy and appeal of nonviolence was not shaken by the events of Convention Week. "What *was* called into question," he said, "was the whole 'coalition' approach to public witness—the idea that you should go along with anyone and any methods so long as your goal is the same. One hopeful sign during the week was the realization by many of the participants—who were often a good bit more nonviolent than their leaders—that the means in a demonstration ought to fit the ends. There were a number of examples of spontaneous nonviolent resistance to police pressures, especially late at night after the news media had gone away. One night the police tried to clear Grant Park, and the demonstrators stood together and sang 'The Star-Spangled Banner,' as a witness that they were not going to be alienated from their own country."

Kale Williams is so concerned with the proper conduct of nonviolent direct action because he explicitly rejects what he calls "the moral calculus"—the reasoning process that men use to determine what amount of human suffering would be an acceptable price for bringing into existence this or that brand of Utopia. As a convinced Quaker—he officially joined Chicago's 57th Street Meeting in 1967—he believes that violence necessarily involves the exploitation and degradation of other individuals, and that therefore acts of violence can *never* contribute, any more than slavery or famine can, to the improvement of the human condition.

PART III

COMMUNITY

❖ ❖ ❖

A VALUABLE PROTOTYPE

ONE of the inspirational anecdotes regularly cited in pacifist literature concerns an American Quaker named Joseph Hoag, who traveled intrepidly through the South during the War of 1812, speaking out at public meetings against both war and slavery. One day in the summer of 1813 he found himself in Knoxville, Tennessee, expounding the Quaker peace testimony to an Army general who had accused local Friends of cowardice for failing to join in the common defense against an anticipated Indian attack. When Hoag had finished making a case for conscientious objection, the general admitted that he had been wrong about the sincerity of the Quaker noncombatants. A bystander who had overheard the entire exchange between the man of war and the man of peace turned to the latter and said, "Well, stranger, if all the world were of your mind, I would turn in and follow after." To which Hoag replied: "Then thou has a mind to be the last man in the world to be good. I have a mind to be one of the first, and set the rest an example."

Aside from the self-righteous tone—an occupational hazard of evangelists—Hoag's rejoinder makes good sense and good morals. Instead of being depressed by the odds against him, he is clearly exhilarated at the thought of being a trail-breaker for mankind in a glorious new adventure. The trouble is, according to their own testimony, Hoag's predecessors felt exactly the same way for exactly the same reason—and so have most of his successors. It is all very well for individual pacifists to keep bolstering their spirits by thinking of themselves as pioneers. But no

ON DOING GOOD

one can look into the history of organized peace movements in this country * without experiencing a repeated sensation of *déjà vu*—and a mounting frustration. In each generation, there is a lively debate between pacifists and nonpacifists about the proper relation of ends and means in the struggle for a better world. Neither side lacks decency or energy or passion. All that is missing is a sense of continuity. The same old debating points —like the comment addressed to Joseph Hoag, or some variant of the familiar challenge, "What would you do if a lunatic attacked your wife and baby?"—are raised afresh and wrangled over. It is as if every quarrel over military strategy were to begin with a serious consideration of the stone ax, or every theological dispute with the question, "Can an omnipotent God make a rock so heavy He can't lift it?" And after each round of the debate, both the protagonists and the antagonists of pacifism are swept away by a new round of war—and their successors start all over again from scratch. Apparently, each generation must discover for itself even the most elementary strengths and weaknesses of the pacifist viewpoint, a condition which virtually ensures that the debate will never get beyond the elementary stage.

One of the rare exceptions to this sad record is the zigzag line of descent that can be traced from the early nineteenth-century nonresistance movement in America to the nonviolent followers of Martin Luther King, Jr.—by way of the example and writings of Count Leo Tolstoy and Mohandas Gandhi. The well-documented story of the rise and fall of the movement founded by William Lloyd Garrison, who ardently espoused both pacifism and abolition, offers illuminating parallels to the Quaker tradition of nonviolence, and to the fate of the antiwar coalition in the United States today.

Although military conscription in the modern sense is usually

* As surveyed in the recent definitive volume, *Pacifism in the United States* by Peter Brock (1968).

said to have begun in Revolutionary France in 1798, Western society has always treated the transition from civilian life to soldiering as a perfectly natural, even desirable rite of manhood. Outside of a few special enclaves like Pennsylvania and Rhode Island, this was just as true in the New World as it had been in the Old. Young men who preferred not to kill people (or even to *learn* how to kill people) were required to run a gauntlet of legal and extralegal pressures, ranging from fines and imprisonment to various forms of social ostracism. While the idea of a standing army was considered vaguely un-American until comparatively recently, every able-bodied man in the American colonies was expected to fulfill his duty to the colonial (later the state) militias. Boys born into the so-called "historic peace churches"—Quakers, Mennonites, Brethren—had the advantage of belonging to an accepted subculture that did not equate virility with violence. But aside from their common refusal to take part in military ventures, the three denominations disagreed among themselves on the proper pacifist response to the demands of society at large. What the Mennonites and the Brethren asked primarily was to be left in peace to devote their lives to Christ in their chosen way. Reforming the rest of the fallen world was not their vocation. For them, the state was at best a necessary evil; and if fines or commutation fees were the price of exemption from military training and service, they gladly paid up, on the principle of rendering Caesar his due in order to be excused from the world's dirty business. From the beginning, the Quakers took a different tack; they not only declined to bear arms, they also insisted that the secular government *recognize* the supremacy of the individual conscience in this matter. To make their witness unmistakable, and to demonstrate that the state, for all its power, could not coerce a man's conscience, the Quakers preferred to go to jail or have their property seized in distraint rather than pay their fines.

The reason for Quaker obstinacy on this point is subtle but

crucial. Even during the long quietist period, the Society of Friends had too much respect for the "proper" role of the state in human affairs (regulating commerce, establishing courts of law, convening representative legislatures) to acquiesce in its abuse. The Quakers held that bad laws and bad states could be improved by good men acting under the guidance of the Inner Light, and they believed that the state ideally deserved the allegiance of all God-fearing men. But the state could *not* demand that a citizen place his allegiance to man's law above God's law. Maintaining the proper relation between these two jurisdictions was as important to the Quakers as the principle of nonviolence itself, and to pay the state for the "privilege" of not bearing arms was to stand this relation on its head.

The early Quakers had exhorted one another to "speak Truth to power." Wherever compulsory military service was in effect, Friends repeatedly petitioned the authorities to grant an unconditional exemption to *all* men—Quakers and non-Quakers—whose scruples prevented them from bearing arms. In America, as elsewhere, these petitions were mostly in vain; the penalties for noncompliance with the militia laws remained on the books. Ironically, the one thing that their persistent lobbying did manage to establish, in the eyes of many Americans, was the sincerity of the Quakers' own antiwar scruples. The Quakers' peculiarities were so well known, and their other civic virtues so well established, that their abstention from military service could easily be tolerated by the authorities. By the middle of the nineteenth century, American Quakers had been virtually granted the status of a privileged minority. In many areas local magistrates applied the provisions of the militia laws less stringently to Quakers. A few states (Massachusetts among them!) went so far as to excuse Quakers by name from the general muster of able-bodied men. Given the temper of the times, such special treatment can be seen as a triumph (however limited in scope) for Quaker persistence. But it was also a special humiliation for a group that had once sounded a moral clarion to awaken other men's consciences. The Quakers of mid-nineteenth-century America were well on their way to becoming domesticated gad-flies, acting out (with official permission) precisely those ideals of Christian Civilization that the secular authorities found it necessary to defend on the battlefield. As long as the Religious Society of Friends accepted this role, there was little likelihood that "birthright Friends"—as all those born into Quaker families were called—would make any original contribution to the theory or practice of pacifism.

And in fact the driving force behind the burgeoning peace movements in the United States in the early 1800's did not come from the ranks of the organized peace churches but from men and women who had rediscovered for themselves the radical Christian ideal of pacifism, and who struggled to perfect their grasp of that ideal in an uncomprehending and hostile world. Although in many ways their struggle resembled that of the early Quaker apostles, a crucial difference in approach soon became apparent. Like William Lloyd Garrison, who founded both the New England Anti-Slavery Society (1832) and the New England Non-Resistance Society (1838), the radical pacifists of this period were also the most ardent abolitionists. This meant that they were faced from the very beginning with the problem of how to wage an effective fight against oppression in society while remaining true to their peace principles. The problem was most acute for those Garrisonians who chose to place a literal interpretation on the Biblical injunction, "Resist not evil." Known as the "ultra" peace men, they believed that the use of force could not be justified even to restrain drunkards, lunatics, and dangerous criminals; and they abstained from *all* politi-cal activity—even when directed against militarism and slaveholding—because they felt that civil government was irredeemably tainted with the spirit of war and violence. Unlike the Quakers, the ultras did not vote in local, state, or federal elections because, as one of their chief polemicists put it, "A *bullet* is in every ballot . . . they are inseparable, as the government is now constituted." The fact that the Quakers who collaborated with the civil government often did so as part of their efforts to aid the Indians, or reform the penal system, or expand the legally recognized rights of conscience, only made them more suspect in the eyes of the ultras. The most zealous Garrisonians were not interested in reform or reconciliation. Having renounced all weapons but the power to move men's souls by moral exhortation and denunciation, they demanded an *immediate* end to slavery, rather than the gradualist approach favored by most Quaker abolitionists. And there was no Quaker mildness in their impatient rhetoric. If the Word was to be their only weapon, the ultras were determined to make it felt; they explicitly condemned the Quakers' traditional "inoffensiveness" toward persons as a luxury that the nonresistant abolitionist could not afford.

As time went on and the forces of "error and prejudice," represented by the Southern slaveholders, refused to yield to the rhetorical cannonade, Garrison and his followers had no alternative but to keep firing away at an ever wider range of targets. Their denunciations of the proponents of compromise grew almost as heated as their attacks on the slave power itself. The gradualists might argue feebly for a political solution that would bring emancipation without bloodshed—possibly through some form of remuneration for slave-owners, along the British precedent—but this became an increasingly unpopular position. While the ultras continued to eschew violence, their explosive sermons helped to convince a growing number of abolition-minded Northerners that only a holocaust could cleanse the nation of the evil of slaveholding.

COMMUNITY

With the passage of the Fugitive Slave Act of 1850, the debate concerning ends and means in the antislavery movement suddenly became more than academic. Armed bounty hunters appeared in the streets of Northern cities, searching for runaway slaves who could now be forcibly returned to a life of servitude in the South. To defend the runaways, the more militant abolitionists began organizing their own vigilante bands. For those remaining abolitionists with scruples about the use of force, the time of decision had clearly come. A very few of the ultras clung to the view that Christ's injunction against violence permitted *no* exceptions—not even when the agents of oppression scavenged for human game in the shadow of the church steeple. And there were other Garrisonians who publicly recanted their pacifism for the duration of the emergency.* But these extreme reactions were not typical. Again, most of the ultras followed Garrison's example in maintaining a strict *personal* pacifism, while rallying all decent nonpacifists to the fight for immediate abolition. There was a certain bitter logic implicit in this position, and to their credit, the Garrisonians did not flinch from pursuing it: "Although non-resistance holds human life in all cases inviolable," Garrison himself wrote, "yet it is perfectly consistent for those professing it to petition, advise, and strenuously urge a pro-war government to abolish slavery solely by the war-power." One of Garrison's closest associates, a man who had earlier denounced any attempt to work for a political solution to the slavery question ("The American nation is a MURDERER" . . . "The blood of murdered millions cries out against all existing national organizations") now felt justified in exhorting his

* In explaining why his ultra peace principles simply did not apply to the battle between pro-slavery and free soil settlers in "Bleeding Kansas" in 1855, one Garrisonian wrote: "When I live with men made in God's image I will never shoot them; but these pro-slavery Missourians are demons from the bottomless pit, and may be shot with impunity."

125

fellow-citizens with these words: "It is the duty of the people and States of the North to invade slaveholding States to free the slaves, and annihilate the power that enslaves them." All abolitionists who had not already renounced warfare on religious principles were openly invited to apply the "torch and sabre" to this "God-appointed work."

The same ultras who had once criticized the Quakers for collaborating with the civil government now turned the argument around to defend their outright war-mongering. Their goal, they said, was merely to see the inevitable violence put to a good purpose; was this any different from the Quakers' acceptance of a police force and punitive courts of law during times of peace? Those Quakers who upheld their sect's traditional peace testimony replied that the restraint of criminals in the name of the law was totally different in theory and practice from the bloody *duello* of mass warfare; that civilization was inconceivable without a government based on law, and that working nonviolently to perfect civil government was the proper way to bring about a just society.

The vast majority of decent men in the North who deplored slavery were not pacifists, of course. But they still had to come to terms with the prospect of a holy war against the South. Their point of view on the eve of the conflict was perhaps best summed up by that clear voice of New England Transcendentalism, Henry David Thoreau. Despite his hatred for all forms of coercion—legal and moral, as well as physical—and his well-known opposition to the Mexican War, Thoreau nevertheless enunciated the classic argument for the moral uses of violence in a speech addressed to his neighbors on October 30, 1859, a few days after John Brown's raid at Harpers Ferry:

> It was his peculiar doctrine [Thoreau said of John Brown] that a man has a perfect right to interfere by force with the slaveholder, in order to rescue the slave. *I agree with him.* . . .

126

I do not wish to kill nor to be killed, but I can foresee circumstances in which both these things would be by me unavoidable.

One such circumstance, Thoreau indicated, was when all other methods had failed to bring about the triumph of a "righteous cause."

When the issue is phrased in these terms—the freedom of four million slaves versus a stubborn adherence to antiwar scruples —it is not hard to see why so many decent men, of whatever persuasion, came to agree with Thoreau. In contrast to the Garrisonians (who urged other people to do what they themselves refused to do) and to the traditional peace sectaries (who appeared all too willing to sacrifice the well-being of others to the demands of an abstract conscience), Thoreau seems to be both compassionate and practical. Rather than tolerate the prolonged suffering of innocents, he chooses to ignore his own delicate feelings. Conscience, properly grounded in reality, leads him *into* battle.

Thoreau's Quaker contemporaries were hardly immune to such sentiments. Two young Friends from Iowa actually took part in John Brown's famous foray, and a number of their coreligionists joined the Northern army as soon as war was declared. Writing to a prominent Friend (Mrs. Eliza P. Gurney) in the fall of 1864, President Abraham Lincoln offered this shrewd appraisal of the plight of all antislavery pacifists during the Civil War:

> Your people have had, and are having, a very great trial. On principle and faith opposed to both war and oppression, they can only practically oppose oppression by war. In this hard dilemma some have chosen one horn and some the other.

Lincoln's expression of sympathy for Quakers who chose not to fight was obviously genuine; whenever possible, he issued pardons for members of the Society who ran afoul of the federal conscription laws. Nevertheless, some Quakers (including Mrs. Gurney) found it necessary to challenge the President's assertion that making war could be a practical—much less the "only" practical—way to oppose oppression. Even as the guns blazed, they kept insisting that one evil ought not to be eliminated by recourse to another evil; that it was as unthinkable to end slavery by waging mass war as it would be to end war by instituting mass slavery.

Decent men like Thoreau and Lincoln are never insensible to the pacifist argument. When they go to war, it is with a heavy heart, and only after they have assured themselves, by use of the moral calculus, that the amount of human suffering inflicted will be an acceptable price to pay for the triumph of such a righteous cause. In the meantime, they see their duty as preserving as much decency as possible until peace can be re-established. The only trouble with this policy (from their own point of view) is that the price of victory has a way of getting out of hand. After adding up the number of combat casualties (a million dead and wounded on both sides), estimating the misery directly traceable to the devastation of the countryside, and reviewing the hundred-year legacy of the conflict in terms of the suffering of innocents—black and white, North and South—an impartial moral accountant might be excused for wondering *which* variety of abolitionist was more willing to sacrifice the well-being of others to the demands of conscience.*

* Implicit in the Quakers' position is the faith that slavery in the United States could have been abolished without bloodshed, perhaps not as quickly but with far less painful consequences for all concerned. No analogy can be completely satisfactory, but the example most frequently cited (at the time and ever since) is that of the British Empire. In 1833 Parliament passed legislation providing for complete emancipation, following a period of "apprenticeship," for some 800,000 black slaves in the West Indian colonies. A feature of the law was financial compensation—totaling

As for the debate between the doctrinaire Quakers and the doctrinaire Garrisonians, it would be an exercise in futility to try to judge which side remained truer to its peace principles during the war years. Faced with the same "hard dilemma," each could claim a certain consistency in word and deed, and each could score debating points against the other. But one thing is certain: without abolition as a rallying point, the non-resistant movement never revived after 1865, while the Society of Friends continued to provide a refuge for a radical peace testimony in a nation otherwise dominated by the spirit of triumphant militarism.

The survival of pacifist sentiment among American Friends cannot be explained simply by the fact that the Society was a religious sect with rigid rules of discipline enforceable by the threat of disownment. Other religious sects in America had chosen to abandon their once rigid peace principles under far less trying circumstances; and the rules of discipline within the Society of Friends were not, in fact, enforced very stringently during the Civil War. With abolitionist sympathies so widespread in the Society, very few of the young Friends who took part in the war were disowned by their Monthly Meetings. Instead, they were asked to make an "acknowledgment of error" on their return. Through this form of compromise, the Monthly Meetings tacitly recognized the difficulty of the moral choice faced by the "fighting Quakers," while reaffirming the Society's basic orientation toward the Peaceable Kingdom.

It may be that the key to the survival of Quaker pacifism—even today when the matter is left ultimately to the individual conscience—lies in that tradition of Quaker "inoffensiveness" which the Garrisonians ridiculed. Although Garrison and his fol-

£20,000,000—for the slave-owners. By the end of the next decade, slaves in all British possessions had been set free, without precipitating a major upheaval.

lowers held that the Mosaic law of an "eye for an eye and a tooth for a tooth" had been superseded by the Christian injunction to "love thine enemy," their rhetoric owed more to the Old Testament prophets than to the Sermon on the Mount. Certainly the ultras failed to maintain a distinction between the evil that men do and the men themselves. By contrast, the Society of Friends, whatever its other inconsistencies, has held firmly to a view of man that encourages reconciliation rather than revenge, no matter what has gone before.

In inheriting this concern, the American Friends Service Committee has also inherited the problem of reconciling an impatient social conscience with an abiding commitment to nonviolence. The same internal conflicts that tore apart the Garrisonian movement have served to attract to the Committee men like Stewart Meacham, a relatively late convert to Quakerism and pacifism, who has headed the Peace Education Division since 1960. As peace secretary, Meacham has been a vigorous and successful advocate of A.F.S.C. participation in broadly based antiwar coalitions, alongside groups whose motives for opposing American military ventures are often far removed from the Quakers' humanitarian and religious concerns. Yet he has remained a respected spokesman for the radical pacifist position —perhaps all the more respected because of his acknowledged difficulties in coming to, and keeping, the faith.

He was born in 1910 in Birmingham, Alabama, where his father was a Presbyterian minister with strong Fundamentalist leanings. After graduating from Davidson College, he enrolled at Louisville Presbyterian Theological Seminary in the fall of 1931. Even at Davidson (which was still, in his words, "very Old South Ivy League") he had begun to have doubts about the relevance of his Fundamentalist beliefs in a world of widespread social unrest and injustice. During his first year at Louisville, he

found himself drawn to one of the seminary's "radical" profes-
sors, an able expounder of the doctrine of nonsectarian Christian pacifism, which had had a rebirth of sorts in the decade following the First World War. "We had a little discussion group
that met in the evenings," Meacham recalled. "The professor
wasn't a spellbinding lecturer, but he spoke with quiet conviction about the symbolism of the Cross, and it suddenly dawned
on me what he was talking about. I had always thought of the
Cross as having to do with the cleansing of sin, as functioning in
a *priestly* way. Now I saw it suddenly as a *way of life*—I saw
the possibility of accepting any violence that might be directed
at me and attempting to transform it into something else by a
radically different response."

For Meacham, this revelation was personally liberating. Now,
for the first time, he felt that it was "consistent" with his religious beliefs to tackle social problems like unemployment and
the equitable redistribution of wealth. Looking around for suitable outlets, he joined a local community improvement group
made up of concerned clergy and philanthropically inclined
businessmen, and in the fall of 1932 he rang doorbells and
handed out campaign literature for Norman Thomas, who was
running for President on the Socialist Party ticket.

Then he came across Reinhold Niebuhr's newly published
book, *Moral Man and Immoral Society,* and experienced another kind of conversion. "Niebuhr attacked the easy assumptions of the kind of Christian pacifism that I had only recently
embraced. The book pointed out that social problems were essentially problems of power; and that pacifists had to relearn
the old truth that the social dimension of Christian love is
justice—which is *not* identical with personal love. Justice, according to Niebuhr, is brought about by a balance of power
among contending social interests. Since we live in a violent

world, the use of violence is not to be ruled out in the effort to achieve this balance—although we ought to choose the less violent, rather than the more violent alternatives."

Within a short time, Meacham had developed a "quiet cynicism" about the committee of "naïve do-gooders" he had been working with. It was quite clear to him now that what the unemployed needed was not handouts, but *power*. In the fall of 1933, he transferred to Union Theological Seminary in New York where Niebuhr was teaching. An ardent disciple of the new social gospel, Meacham soon became involved in the left wing of the city labor movement, marching alongside striking workers and taking part in endless discussions of Marxist theory and practice. Through it all, he was still determined to become a Presbyterian minister and radicalize the church from within.

On his return to Birmingham the following spring, he was appointed assistant pastor of "about the richest church in town." Since his superior was away for most of the summer, Meacham had a relatively free hand. Among his innovations was a Sunday-evening discussion forum; two of the first speakers were the head of the local chapter of the N.A.A.C.P. and a union organizer for the United Mine Workers. His choice of speakers caused a predictable stir among the more conservative parishioners, but the evenings passed without major incident until he invited a *Negro* union organizer—a combination which was apparently too much for the congregation's largest contributor. The forum was abruptly canceled, and Meacham found himself in the ranks of unemployed Presbyterian pastors.

After spending the winter in the unlikely capacity of a guard with the Brinks armored-car company, he was assigned by the state presbytery to a small church in a working-class district of Birmingham. He had kept up his union connections, and was now pressed into service as unofficial chaplain to the local labor movement. "The mine union was the first statewide organization

in Alabama to be integrated. There was lots of brotherhood feeling; the locals met in churches, and sang union words set to
hymn tunes." The next year there was an outbreak of beatings
and floggings in Birmingham; the victims were all connected
with the union in one way or another. "Someone tipped me off
that I was going to get beat up, and a friend of mine talked me
into carrying his gun, a .22 revolver. I kept it for a few days in
the little pocket under the windshield in my model-A Ford. All
this time I was walking around with a mixture of pacifist and
nonpacifist beliefs in my head. I hadn't really been apprehensive
before I got the gun, but once I armed myself, I started looking
up and down the street before stepping from the car, and glanc-
ing behind me when I entered a meeting. I thought to myself,
Now I'm scared stiff. So I gave back the gun, and I felt better
right away. I was *personally* a pacifist again—but I still believed that violence might be necessary in achieving social justice."

Meacham's growing interest in trade unions as the "vanguard
of the future" led him to take a job on the West Coast with the
National Labor Relations Board in 1937. "It may sound strange
today, but the N.L.R.B. was very idealistic in those early years.
We felt we were transforming society by bringing about a new
balance of power." When the war came, Meacham found no difficulty in supporting it as a "just" war. "Hitler was a threat to
everything good in the world. If I hadn't had a deferred job, I
would have gone into the army rather than ask for C.O. status."
But as the fighting continued, he began to be dismayed by the
attitude of selfishness and cynicism that he saw spreading
through the labor movement; although the unions were stronger
than anyone had dared hope in the thirties, they owed their new
strength not to any transformation of society, but to the patron-
age of government officials who controlled the war economy.

At the suggestion of a friend in Los Angeles, Meacham went

one Sunday to a Congregationalist church whose minister considered himself a Christian pacifist of the old school. On this
particular morning, the minister read from the pulpit an honor
role of those members of his congregation who were absent in
the service of their country. Included were members of the three
military branches, employees of various civilian agencies (like
the N.L.R.B.) and a handful of conscientious objectors, both
those who were performing government-approved alternative
service *and* those who were sitting in prison for noncooperation
with the draft law. The impact on Meacham was profound. "I
had forgotten that there were people willing to sacrifice so much
for that principle. I didn't exactly walk out of the church a strict
pacifist, but I began heading back in that direction." The news
of Hiroshima jolted him the rest of the way. "I had begun to
feel increasingly uncomfortable with the doctrine of the less violent alternative. Now I saw that a commitment to *any* violence
in the name of justice was a treacherous thing: It might lead
logically to dropping the Bomb, and I didn't want to take any
part in that logic."

After the war, Meacham accepted an executive position with
the Amalgamated Clothing Workers of America, and he and his
wife moved east to Ridgewood, N.J. "We started casting about
for a church and found this little Quaker Meeting nearby. I had
been getting more humanistic and less theological in my approach to religion over the years; and I felt so much a Quaker
already that I was reluctant to join the meeting in a formal
sense because it seemed like a contradiction." His formal association with the American Friends Service Committee began in
1957 when he was named director of the Labor International Affairs Program. In the years since, he has become a familiar
figure in the peace movement here and abroad. He was a co-
chairman of the New Mobilization Committee to End the War
in Vietnam; he has flown to Hanoi to help arrange the release

of captured American pilots; he has argued over the prerequisites for a European detente with a Soviet "peace delegation" in Moscow; and he has turned out pamphlets and speeches opposing military conscription in general and the insanity of a foreign policy based on a nuclear balance of terror.

Although most of the efforts of the A.F.S.C. Peace Education Division are focused on specific issues which also attract a broad range of nonpacifist support, the Service Committee has periodically tried to relate these issues to the traditional Quaker peace testimony. The most ambitious attempt in recent years was the publication in 1967 of a pamphlet entitled, "In Place of War: An Inquiry into Nonviolent National Defense." The purpose of the pamphlet, prepared by a ten-man working party under the auspices of the Peace Education Division, is to offer a pacifist alternative to all the usual concepts of disarmament—bi-, uni-, and multilateral. Citing a number of widely scattered historical precedents and drawing heavily on the theoretical work of a group of English pacifists, the authors of the pamphlet propose a course of action known as "transarmament," whereby a major power like the United States gradually junks its war machine while simultaneously creating a system of "civilian defense," based on the thorough grounding of a large part of its population in the techniques of nonviolent resistance. The authors point out that a large nation defended only in this manner could never inadvertently provoke its neighbors into aggression; and they contend that a nation with such a ready-made resistance movement would, in fact, be highly immune to invasion, since a potential aggressor would find the logistics of occupation almost prohibitive. They concede that a hypothetical madman might not be deterred by such considerations—but then the same madman would probably not be impressed by the chilling calculus of nuclear deterrence either. And if such a madman were loosed on the world, hell-bent on conquest or nuclear annihilation, the chances for national survival (not to mention the survival of civilization and the human race itself) could only be improved if the response from the other powers were nonviolent.

As outlined in the pamphlet, the ideal civilian-defense network would combine the organizational genius of the various underground resistance forces in World War II with the spiritual fervor of the protest movements led by Gandhi and Martin Luther King. In the event of invasion, the nonviolent defenders would try to wean the occupying troops away from the invader's policies by a "conscious and deliberate" campaign of fraternization stressing a common humanity. At the same time, through selective noncooperation, the defenders would seek to deny the invader any material benefits from his conquest. In all their actions, the defenders would accept the possibility of martyrdom the way good soldiers accept the possibility of death in battle, but there would be nothing passive about their stance. Aggressive impulses and the desire for revenge would find outlets in the nonviolent derring-do of civilian defense—operating radio transmitters, organizing strikes and sit-ins in the face of military repression, and the like. The authors insist that they are not calling for a nation of saints:

> During World War II millions of people on both sides, *having accepted the premises of violent struggle,* displayed tremendous courage, made great sacrifices and endured unbelievable suffering without yielding to the enemy . . . On what basis can it be claimed that a people, *having once accepted the premises of nonviolent struggle,* would be unable to rise to the same heights of endurance and fortitude?

Yet the tone of the pamphlet is not at all optimistic. Although the authors note that "civilian defense is based upon confidence in nonviolent methods, rather than upon a belief in nonviolence in principle," they seem doubtful about convincing significant numbers of people that a nonviolent struggle has at least as good a chance to succeed as a violent one. They keep stressing the tentative nature of their proposal; they call for more research; they confess their uncertainty on a number of crucial points (such as the need for secrecy in conducting resistance operations, and the use of noninjurious sabotage directed against the invader's military establishment). Meacham, who was a member of the working party that produced "In Place of War," is quick to admit that the pamphlet "did not write easily. Obviously, we haven't solved the problems of *corporate* nonviolence, which is a much more complex thing than personal pacifism. I may find it quite easy to come to a personal decision to resist an aggressor nonviolently. And others may join me out of personal conviction. But what about those who won't go along? How are they affected by my decision? How am I affected by theirs? How many people in a community have to be convinced before corporate nonviolence can work at all? I know I would feel reluctant to sit down and argue nonviolent resistance with the black militants, for instance. They've had more life-experience in it than I have. Their most articulate spokesmen were boldly nonviolent a few years ago, and they got their heads beat. I've been a Fundamentalist, a Christian Pacifist, a Niebuhrian, a humanist—and I'm not about to change again. But I think we have to be extremely modest in talking about what we think will work for others."

Meacham's prescription of extreme modesty is a far cry from the infectious confidence of early Quaker apostles like George Fox and William Penn, who built radically new institutions to embody the Truth they had seen revealed. But founding an institution in the name of certain fundamental principles, and keeping it consistent with those principles over the years, are two entirely different matters. Like most liberal institutions, the future health of the Service Committee will depend on its con-

tinued ability to reinterpret its principles in the light of new
challenges—even if this means rejecting some cherished illusions
about its own past. So far, not even the Committee's stand on
conscientious objection has proved to be immune to this process.

As we have seen, American Quakers were quite active in
trying to win legislative approval for the principle of unconditional conscientious objection in the decades prior to the Civil
War. But what they won primarily were special favors for members of the Religious Society of Friends. During the Civil War
itself, both President Lincoln and Secretary of War Stanton
were especially solicitous about the fortunes of individual Quakers arrested for failure to comply with the stringent federal conscription laws (which originally exempted only those who hired
substitutes or paid a $300 commutation fee). While some Quak-
ers did suffer terribly for their conscientious refusal to train and
fight, those Friends whose cases reached the desk of either Lincoln or Stanton were usually paroled or furloughed for the duration without further punishment. In 1864 the conscription law
was amended to let members of the traditional peace sects fulfill
their obligations (on the approval of the Secretary of War) by
caring for the sick or wounded in hospitals, or by working with
newly freed blacks. Some Quakers seized this opportunity to
perform noncombatant service; others denounced it as being no
different in principle from the payment of a commutation fee.
But hardly anyone in the Society of Friends commented on the
fact that the federal government had singled out the conscience
of certain religious sectaries for special consideration.

When the first Selective Service Act was passed following the
United States' entry into World War I, a similarly restricted option of noncombatant service was offered to adherents of "any
well recognized religious sect . . . whose existing creed or principles forbid its members to participate in war in any form."
The American Friends Service Committee came into being to

help young Quakers exercise this option. The premise of its founders was that, *especially in wartime,* a pacifist should engage in an active witness of humanitarian principles. But some of those who were eligible for this form of alternative service— and many who were not—refused to cooperate with the Selective Service authorities. These "absolutists" were not draft-dodgers by any conceivable definition of that term; rather they were men who went out of their way to inform the authorities that they would not become cogs (even noncombatant cogs) in the machinery of conscription. Nor were their views so alien to the temper of the time. Even in the wartime Congress, the Selective Service bill had stirred passionate opposition from legislators who had never been known for radical pacifist sympathies: "Must we Prussianize ourselves in order to win democracy for the people of the world?" (Rep. James F. Byrnes of South Carolina); "It is as repugnant to democracy as any despotic principle which can be conceived" (Sen. Charles F. Thomas of Colorado); "Its essential feature is that of involuntary servitude" (Sen. James A. Reed of Mississippi). But these sentiments were all expressed *before* the bill became law. The penalties for persisting in such views after the Congressional majority had spoken were severe: all in all, 504 conscientious noncooperators were court-martialed and 345 were given prison terms averaging 16½ years; 142 were sentenced to life imprisonment, and seventeen were condemned to death. (None of the death sentences were carried out; the remaining C.O.'s in prison were pardoned by President Roosevelt in 1933.)

In the summer of 1940, Congress began debating a proposal for the first peacetime draft in the nation's history. Again, there was strong opposition in both houses. Representative Jerry Voorhis of California, who was to lose his seat in 1946 to a young Republican challenger named Richard Nixon, made this prophetic statement: "Believe me, gentlemen, it is going to be difficult to ever repeal such a measure once you get it established, for you will have made of your military establishment one of the greatest economic factors in your whole country."

Friends joined other pacifist groups in lobbying against the draft. They also asked that if such legislation *were* passed, the provision for religious conscientious objectors be made nondenominational. (Over the years, Quakers had formed a smaller and smaller percentage of the total number of conscientious objectors in the United States.)

The Quakers' opposition to the passage of the draft bill proved futile. But partly because the armed forces did not want to be bothered with all those recalcitrant C.O.'s again, the new law did exempt from "combatant training and service" any person who "by reason of religious training and belief is conscientiously opposed to participation in war in any form." Such men were expected to perform noncombatant service in one of the military branches, or to engage in "work of national importance under civilian direction" in what came to be known as the Civilian Public Service program. Some 12,000 conscientious objectors, representing two hundred different religious sects and denominations, eventually came under the jurisdiction of Civilian Public Service. The C.P.S. program, which centered around large work camps in the style of the Civilian Conservation Corps, was administered and financed at government request by the American Friends Service Committee, the Mennonite Central Committee and the Brethren Service Committee. But the Selective Service Administration remained the sole arbiter of the "conscientiousness" of a man's objection to war, and nearly six thousand noncooperators went to prison during World War II for failure to accept Selective Service rulings. About three-quarters of these were Jehovah's Witnesses who had been denied the ministerial status which their sect claimed for all its members; the rest were absolutists of one persuasion or another.

Even before the C.P.S. program came to an end in 1947, the American Friends Service Committee began to have second thoughts about its own close collaboration with the machinery of conscription. After V-J Day, the Board of Directors announced that the A.F.S.C. would not undertake a similar administrative role in the future, and in 1948 the Committee joined the wider Quaker community in reaffirming its opposition to *all* forms of conscription. But A.F.S.C. counselors continued to provide information and impartial aid to all young men—Quaker and non-Quaker—who were interested in the legal channels of conscientious objection: the 1-A-0 classification (for men whose consciences permitted them to perform noncombatant service in some branch of the armed forces), and the 1-0 classification (for men who were willing to perform some kind of government-approved alternative service outside the armed forces, such as working for the Service Committee itself).

The growth of the draft resistance movement in the late sixties added a new dimension to the concept of conscientious objection. Now there were large numbers of young men who, without being pacifists or even religiously inclined, simply did not want to fight in an unpopular war in Vietnam. While they certainly did not fit the stereotype of the old-style draft-dodger, they were not as ready to go to jail as the old-style noncooperator. Ineligible for the standard C.O. exemptions, they saw their options as including migration to Canada, going underground in this country, lying to the authorities about mental and physical disabilities, and disrupting the Selective Service machinery itself. Those who were attracted to the last option formed the nucleus of the new breed of absolutists, who began to insist that *no one* should collaborate in any way with an evil system like the draft. For the most zealous, even accepting the legal penalties for not registering was a form of collaboration. Anything less than total resistance, these new absolutists argued, was playing into the hands of the military establishment, which was able to impose its will on the nation only because the people were not aware of how basically coercive and undemocratic the draft was. Although many of these total resisters had taken their first steps toward conscientious objection with the guidance of an A.F.S.C. (or A.F.S.C.-trained) counselor, they now called on the Service Committee to stop temporizing and join the antidraft movement in earnest.

An internal debate began in the Committee on how far a draft counselor could go in helping an individual evade military service, and how far the Committee itself should go in publicly supporting the newly organized resistance groups. One of the most forceful statements came from Ben Seaver, the peace education secretary for the San Francisco region, who had been counseling young men of draft age since 1940. At a staff conference in January 1968, Seaver said he now believed that the American Friends Service Committee and the Quakers in general had been the beneficiaries of "*extreme* discrimination" on the part of the federal government ever since the enactment of the first Selective Service law:

> "We have intellectually condemned conscription as a fundamentally evil system contrary to basic human rights. But when it became law we somehow accommodated ourselves to it provided it allowed us an out. . . . We accepted things which, when you examine them, turned out to be unbelievable: That we should accept the right of the government not only to define religion, which seems to be forbidden in the First Amendment, but also that we should allow the government to decide that only those who met this definition had a conscience that was worth considering; that others didn't have a conscience . . ."

Seaver was referring to Selective Service Form 150, which all prospective C.O.'s had to fill out, and which included such

key queries as: "1. Do you believe in a Supreme Being? ☐
Yes ☐ No. 2. Describe the nature of your belief . . . and
state whether or not your belief in a Supreme Being involves
duties which to you are superior to those arising from any
human relation. 3. Explain how, when, and from whom or
from what source you received the training and acquired the
belief."

Spurred on by Seaver and others who had come to the same
conclusion, the executive committee of the Peace Education
Committee adopted a minute which explicitly rejected the government's role as "lord of conscience," and suggested that the
Service Committee concentrate in the future on rendering "aid
and support" to noncooperators and nonviolent resisters.

This document was submitted to the A.F.S.C. Board of Directors, along with a parallel minute prepared by the Youth Services Division, which declared: "It is increasingly evident that
the deferment system serves the purpose of removing opposition
to the draft. We therefore feel obligated to oppose the system in
its entirety." Both these documents stressed that the Committee
need not withdraw its services and moral support from the thousands of young men who still felt comfortable with the traditional C.O. position. But the clear implication was that the
Committee itself had been all too comfortable with it.

This was a strong charge indeed. In a sense, the directors
were being asked to repudiate a major chapter in the Committee's history—a chapter which some of them, as veterans of Civilian Public Service, had taken part in without shame and even
with a sense of pride and accomplishment. (As orderlies in mental hospitals, for example, Quaker C.O.'s had successfully
introduced nonviolent methods of dealing with violent patients,
and had gone on to organize the National Mental Health Foundation.)

The entire issue of the Committee's attitude toward conscientious objection was placed on the agenda of the 1968 Representative Council, an informal but influential body whose purpose was to bring together members of the Board of Directors, national staff, and delegates from the regional offices. It soon became apparent at this meeting, much to the surprise of some Board members, that draft counselors in the regional offices were already dealing regularly with the new type of draft resister, and even with A.W.O.L. soldiers seeking sanctuary or a passage on the new "Underground Railroad" to Canada.

Some members of the Board were especially bothered by the idea of A.F.S.C. counselors aiding young men who were intent on breaking the law; the Board's policy had always been to support the right of individuals to engage in civil disobedience, but *not* to involve the Committee as a corporate entity in such actions since this might jeopardize the status of unrelated programs with equally high priorities. Another matter of concern was how closely the A.F.S.C. wanted to be identified with a movement whose goals might be compatible with the Committee's, but whose commitment to nonviolence was uncertain, to say the least. And for some people at Representative Council, an even more subtle question was involved: Could it be morally proper for those beyond the reach of the draft law to encourage young C.O.'s to take grave risks that the older men, by definition, could not share?

It is standard operating procedure among Quakers when no consensus emerges from a large meeting to appoint a smaller committee (with all conflicting opinions represented) to continue the discussion on a more intimate plane and report back to the parent body when the conflicts are resolved. Representative Council now charged such a subcommittee with preparing an entirely new minute on conscientious objection and draft counseling. After considering three different drafts from the subcommittee, the Council finally reached consensus on a formula which the Board of Directors later endorsed as the policy of the American Friends Service Committee.

As might be expected, this product of the consensus process was neither a confession of past sins nor an affirmation of business as usual. While carefully noting that the Board did not share "all the views" held by the draft resisters, the minute did say:

> We nevertheless feel a strong sympathy with their resistance to participation in what we have recognized as evil. We are clear in our relation to young men who choose 1-0 or 1-A-0 status under conscription, or who accept legal penalties for refusal to cooperate. Our growing perception of the evil of conscription itself . . . should now lead us to confirm our support of those who refuse cooperation. We should expand our services and review our educational and counseling materials to insure that their moral position is also given due weight. Our counseling should be available to all. We should give our services to any person whose confrontation with military service is direct and open and in the tradition of nonviolence.

This statement obviously fell far short of the objectives of the activists in the regional offices. The oblique reference to "our *growing* perception" was the only hint that the Committee might have been short-sighted in the past. Even those Committee members who helped draft the document agreed that the wording was imprecise. But according to one regional executive secretary, the minute served its primary purpose as a recognition by the somewhat conservative Board that draft-counseling practices had in fact changed, and that the change was in accord with A.F.S.C. principles. For example, there was a young man in the Chicago office who had been hired as a draft counselor a year before; in recent months he had begun devoting part of his time to organizing an independent group called CADRE (Chicago Area Draft Resisters). As a draft counselor with the A.F.S.C., he continued to provide information and guidance to all those who were interested in the legal channels of conscientious objection. As a CADRE organizer, he tried to persuade other young men to take the more extreme resistance position.

The young man's name was Rick Boardman. A native of Acton, Massachusetts, where his parents were members of the local Quaker Meeting, he had registered more or less automatically as a C.O. at the age of eighteen, and then accepted a temporary student deferment to attend Antioch College. In his own words, he "did not identify strongly with political personalities or issues" as an undergraduate. After fulfilling his academic requirements under Antioch's work-study program, he came to Chicago in the fall of 1966 to find a job that would allow him to earn the remaining credits he needed toward his degree, and at the same time satisfy his alternative-service obligation to his hometown draft board. He was certainly not thinking in terms of the resistance movement when he decided to join the Chicago office of the Service Committee as a "peace interne." In fact, he wrote to his draft board in Acton asking for the necessary approval. (At the time, some sixty C.O.'s were doing their alternative service in some capacity or other with the A.F.S.C.) After five months of consideration and a lengthy correspondence, the Acton board finally ruled that a job involving draft counseling could not be considered "suitable civilian work in lieu of military service." Rick was told to reapply when he had found another position.

But by this time, he had done enough draft counseling to have some insight into what he later called the "structural weaknesses" of the conscription machinery. The more he thought about his personal problem, the more it seemed to be a reflection of everything that was wrong with the system. He knew

that because of his family background and education, he would
have no trouble satisfying the draft board's requirements if he
really tried, but it seemed to him that he could do so only by
compromising his own values; that is, by tacitly accepting "the
legitimacy of the system of conscription, and the military for
which conscription exists."

The quotation is from a letter which Rick eventually sent to
his draft board (and to his hometown newspaper as well) explaining why he was returning his draft card and voluntarily
giving up his "elitist 1-0 deferment." He had briefly considered
burning his card in one of the public conflagrations which were
a popular tactic of the resistance movement in its early days.
But after witnessing such a ceremony, he decided that he was
more interested in "provoking people to think about the main issues involved" than in making a symbolic, inflammatory gesture.
In his open letter, dated April 24, 1967, Rick confessed that he
had originally seen no problem of conscience in applying for a
1-0 deferment:

> When my claim as a conscientious objector was recognized I
> was pleased and began to think that perhaps we have a very
> "reasonable" system of conscription after all. I found myself
> thinking that it's a very good system of conscription that "al-
> lows" a man to try to help his fellows to live constructively in-
> stead of destructively. I had failed to stop to question by what
> authority it came to be that a man should have to justify this
> creative inclination to his draft board. I had failed to realize
> that my deferment as a CO was a convenient way by which my
> resistance to conscription and the military (and the resistance of
> thousands like me) was effectively silenced.

To place his act of civil disobedience in a wider context, he
quoted from Gandhi, Thoreau, and Isaac Penington, an early
Quaker apologist who wrote (concerning the "peaceable king-

dom" foretold by prophecy), "Whoever desires to see this lovely state brought forth in the general, must cherish it in the particular."

Rick went on to argue that, contrary to the board's ruling, his work in resisting the draft was very much "in the national interest":

> As one brought up to believe in the American principles of individualism and voluntarism I must reject any system of imposed and involuntary recruitment of manpower, and as one brought up to believe in the basic equality of all people and to respect the law only when it is equally administered to all citizens regardless of race, creed, color, social class or education, I must reject a system of conscription that defers the most fortunate members of society and forces the least fortunate to bear the burden of responsibility and risk in the military.

"I understand," he also wrote, "that by refusing to comply with the Selective Service System I will be breaking the law." As expected, he was indicted for refusing to obey a mandatory work order, found guilty, and sentenced to three years in federal prison.

Rick had identified himself to his draft board as a pacifist, but in a later interview, he amended that to "attempting to become a pacifist." Although he acknowledged the importance of Quaker values in his thinking, he said that he did not consider himself a member of any Quaker Meeting because "membership implies an exclusion of others, and I'm leery of that." As for the Service Committee, he said that he found its attitude toward political and social change generally "more reformist than activist," but the important thing was that "it allows itself to be convinced on occasions." One of these occasions, he felt, was the decision of the Board of Directors to "support the resistance." As he saw it, this was an indication of the path that the Committee would have to pursue in the future: "Away from helping the individual beat the system, to changing the system itself."

The American Friends Service Committee has always prided itself on its ability—despite prior commitments, financial obligations, and administrative complexities—to remain sensitive to an individual act of conscience. Nothing has been more influential in the Committee's evolution than the old Quaker concept of personal "concern." From the beginning, a Friend who was moved to action by the plight of the hungry, the sick, or the exploited in some part of the world would ask for the blessing and material support of his Monthly or Yearly Meeting. The impetus for this so-called Quaker outreach was supposed to come from the individual, who then had the responsibility of convincing his coreligionists not only of the urgency and feasibility of the specific job he had in mind, but also of the sincerity of his concern. As important as the merits of the proposal might be, the collective judgment was ultimately based on impressions of personal integrity that could not be reduced to facts and figures.

Among other things, the Service Committee was set up to institutionalize this procedure, and most of its problems, as well as many of its triumphs, have come from the tensions generated in the course of carrying out such an unlikely assignment. In the early years, the idea was simply to match those who wanted to serve with those who needed help. For Friends who felt moved to undertake some sort of humanitarian service but who had no particular area of concern, the Committee found suitable projects in this country or abroad. Pleas for assistance were never lacking, and while special skills were sometimes needed, more often the work called only for a steady hand, a clear head, and a boundless compassion. Even as the Committee grew in size from a handful of permanent staff to hundreds of full-time employees, this essentially amateur concept of service was retained. For all its interfaith and interracial aspects, the A.F.S.C. was still the agent of social outreach for the Religious Society of Friends; and to lose contact with individual concerns was to risk spiritual stagnation.

The Committee has been especially wary of any long-term commitment which would lock it into the mold of the Professional Welfare Agency (dispensing a regular dole to a permanent clientele) or the General Research Foundation (an interested third party with enough surplus cash to speculate in social progress). As a matter of policy, the Board has taken pains *not* to build up a large endowment, preferring to spend all available funds on current service projects; in the words of one fundraiser, "we feel more comfortable depending on people who know what we are doing *today*."

Annual income has been climbing steadily in recent years, but the increase has not kept pace with increasing costs, much less with the constantly growing demands on A.F.S.C. resources. In the early 1960's, a $3 million windfall in the form of two unusually large bequests was received; in keeping with the "no-endowment" policy, the entire principal was fed into the annual budget over a period of several years. When this windfall was exhausted, the Service Committee was faced with a severe budget squeeze. Coincidentally, an independent consulting firm which had been asked to examine the Committee's fund-raising efforts issued its report to the Board of Directors. After stating that the "A.F.S.C. is the best dollar value of any not-for-profit organization we have ever examined," the consultants nevertheless predicted that the Committee was going to fall behind in the increasingly competitive chase for the "philanthropic dollar" unless it learned to sell itself to large institutional donors like the General Research Foundations (Ford, Rockefeller, and others). To do this, however, the Committee would have to break out of its present pattern of service—"a patchwork quilt of fragmented and diverse activities which are difficult to evaluate in relation to social change." Instead of concentrating on short-range financial plans and programs (the report went on), the staff should begin designing some major projects focused on "issues of national importance" with a "research and evaluation component built in." When these programs begin to show measurable results, the Committee can then "gear its communications program and some of its public relations" to make sure that its role in stimulating social change the nonviolent way is "understood and appreciated by pertinent segments of the population." The report also suggested that a Friendly desire to be "all things to all people" was blurring the Committee's image and interfering with its fund-raising potential: "We find that the literature of A.F.S.C. is too preoccupied with philosophy and not enough with tangible evidence of public service."

The authors of this report were aware that some of their proposals would be distasteful to many people associated with the Committee. But they were also aware of speaking to a widespread concern within the A.F.S.C. family. There are people on the staff today who believe that the traditional Quaker reverence for individual concerns is getting in the way of the more important business of analyzing the needs of American society and shaping programs to meet those needs. These people fear that an organization whose sole guide is "to see what love can do" may spread itself too thin, and in trying to do too much may end up doing far too little. And they argue that the "cutting edge of social change" (a favorite phrase in the A.F.S.C. lexicon) is now to be found in those areas—in the ghettos, among the radical youth—where trained professionals can be much more effective than self-motivated amateurs.

But the cutting edge of social change evidently cuts both ways. There are others on the Committee who think that it is the professional staff—especially the heads of the program divisions in the national office—who are out of touch with the ghettos and the young. In fact, a group of young people working for the Committee recently got together and formed an "uncommittee" to dramatize their sense of alienation from the A.F.S.C. establishment. After shaking up the 1969 Representative Council with a list of "proposals/demands" for a greater say in policymaking—and arguing among themselves over whether even the formation of an "uncommittee" was consistent with their antibureaucratic purpose—the young people disbanded, to continue their protest as concerned individuals. The news that the Board of Directors had already decided to add five new members between the ages of twenty and twenty-seven did not particularly impress the protesters, who pointed out that they had not even been consulted on *that* decision.°

A former executive secretary of the Service Committee once remarked that the main trouble with his colleagues and himself was that "We're caught up in a lot of vested disinterest." Dr. Robert Leopold, a Philadelphia psychiatrist who has acted as a consultant to the A.F.S.C. personnel department since 1958, concurs in this diagnosis, but he is appropriately ambivalent about prescribing a cure. On the one hand, he believes that "the Committee can't get much larger and maintain its present structure"; eventually, major contributors will demand "hard figures" and the Committee will have to recognize that long-range planning, the setting of priorities, and scientific efforts to measure the

° Later, many of the unmembers of the uncommittee were given the opportunity and the funds to operate a summer project of their own choice—an investigation of the inadequacies of federal food-relief programs. At the end of the summer, regular staff members were impressed with the quality of the research and the final report, and the young people in charge of the project were impressed with the need for at least a minimum of budgetary control and other "bureaucratic" procedures.

effectiveness of its work do not necessarily violate its principles. On the other hand, he would not like to see anything interfere with the unique social organism the Committee has evolved into —a continuing experiment proving that people can live together nonviolently and constructively by focusing on individual and consensual concerns. "The A.F.S.C.," he says, "is a valuable prototype of how we must live if we're going to live at all."

The success of this experiment probably depends to a great extent on the careful selection of "like-minded" participants. According to its general recruitment manual, the personnel department recognizes that "It is of vital importance to have individuals whose lives reflect a reconciling and loving spirit. Some A.F.S.C. positions, including most overseas assignments, require complete acceptance of the basic testimonies of pacifism and of the equal worth of all persons." However, Dr. Leopold (who describes himself as "ethnically Jewish" but drawn "ethically and spiritually to Quaker values") goes on to say that "there is a mistaken belief that this is a *nonaggressive* group. Quakers are no less aggressive than other people. Actually, the acceptance of plain-speaking in a group can work to bring out and control aggression. You learn that strong negative feelings can be respected. There is a real parallel here to psychotherapy. You must feel free to say whatever irrational—that is, emotional— thing comes to mind. The system works because people find they *can't* be authoritarian and be effective."

One of the least authoritarian and most effective men on the Committee in recent years has been Gilbert White, who completed a six-year term as chairman of the Board of Directors in the fall of 1969. As chairman, White's job was to articulate the consensus of the Board when he felt that one had been reached, or to suggest that the Board move on when he felt that there was no unity on a particular issue. He had little use for the latter prerogative, since a complete impasse is rare among veterans

153

of the Committee process. But as much as they value unity, Quakers have also learned to be wary of reaching a consensus *too* quickly, since this may mean that not enough divergent points of view were represented in the first place. During White's tenure as chairman, the Board took steps to make itself more responsive to the cross-currents of opinion throughout the Committee (the co-optation of five "under thirty" directors being probably the most controversial of these steps). Of the fifty-seven directors on the 1968–69 Board, twelve were women, three were Negroes, and several were in the awkward category of "youthful but over thirty." The honorary chairman, Henry J. Cadbury, an eminent Biblical scholar and one of the founders of the Committee, was eighty-six years old. There were more educators than lawyers and businessmen combined, a fair representation of housewives and social workers, and a handful of engineers and other professional men.

White himself is a former professor of geography at the University of Chicago and an international authority on the development and conservation of water resources. But he tends to be skeptical about the application of sophisticated planning techniques, such as the systems approach and cost-benefit analysis, to problems of social change: "My personal view is that the Committee does have a responsibility to experiment with these techniques, but having worked for more than thirty years in one of the most advanced disciplines with regards to planning, the experience does not give me much confidence. I'm more familiar with the techniques, and more familiar with their deficiencies. At best, they're crude tools."

In an earlier era, the Quakers used the phrase "weighty Friend" to describe an influential member of a Meeting. In the context of the Service Committee, Gilbert White, a convert to Quakerism, is the very model of a "weighty Friend"—and during the last few years the weight of his opinion has usually fallen on the side of those who see the Committee as essentially a *fellowship* of service, the sum total of hundreds of individual concerns. He has suggested that the Committee decentralize decision-making as far as possible, even if this means surrendering the control of funds (and its jealously guarded reputation for financial integrity) to the people in the field. And just for a change, he would ask the Committee's regular contributors what good works *they* see a need for, instead of merely asking them to support projects already planned or in progress.

Ironically, it was the big budget squeeze during White's chairmanship—a drop of $600,000 in available funds between 1968 and 1969—that gave new impetus to the long-range planners and priority-setters within the A.F.S.C. constituency. A special committee of the Board was set up to determine which programs could be cut back with the least damage, and after an extensive survey it was decided that the top priority should go to "programs that attempt to facilitate social change through nonviolent means." As a result, the ax fell heaviest on the more traditional overseas and youth work—such as cultural exchanges, and other projects aimed largely at the personal enrichment of the participants—while the Peace Education Division suffered hardly at all, and the Community Relations Division was exempted entirely.

For the fiscal year ended September 30, 1968, the A.F.S.C. spent $1,121,313 in Community Relations programs which employed more than sixty full-time staff and touched the lives of thousands of people on the bleak margins (or in the equally uncomfortable fissures) of the Affluent Society. These programs were summed up in the Annual Report as follows:

> Work in metropolitan areas of the North and West to find creative solutions to a broad range of urban problems, particularly housing and education; work to affect the patterns of change in Deep South public schools; community development efforts

with farm laborers, migrants and other rural poor in California and southeastern Pennsylvania; special efforts in the East Coast migrant stream from a base in Florida; community development and leadership training with the American Indian groups in Maine, California, Washington, and Montana; work with released prisoners in California and Iowa.

Actually, the question, "Why *these* particular projects in *these* particular places at *this* particular time?" was a little embarrassing to the more priority-conscious people in the Community Relations Division. The answers were often as varied as the projects themselves. Some projects had been initiated in one of the regional offices by a concerned staff or committee member responding to a local crisis. Others—like the work with the American Indians—reflected traditional Quaker concerns that go back to the days of George Fox and William Penn. And still others—like the efforts at neighborhood organization on Chicago's West Side—resulted from a combination of genuine grassroots pressure, judicious guidance by trained professionals, and the historical accident of the Committee's presence in the community.

The secretary of the Community Relations Division is a former newspaper reporter named Barbara Moffett, who is probably the most influential non-Quaker in the Committee's administrative hierarchy. (She is not a member of any religious denomination.) In the wake of the Kerner Commission's report on urban disorders in the summer of 1967, she prepared a forty-page memorandum entitled "Questions About Our Future," which received a wide distribution in the regions and in the national office. The main question raised in the memo was whether the American Friends Service Committee was willing to play an "important part" in the gigantic national effort needed to solve the domestic crisis. It was suggested that the answer lay in "committing ourselves to a decade or more of large-scale work," and in pinpointing program areas "which, added to our present effort, might provide a traceable impact on social change"— even if this required *doubling* the Community Relations budget.

Despite her penchant for voluminous memo writing, Barbara Moffett has never conceived of the struggle against poverty and racism (nor for that matter, against the A.F.S.C. budget squeeze) in terms of grandiose strategical concepts or sweeping manifestoes. She believes in planning; but from her point of view, a "decade of large-scale work" breaks down almost immediately into a list of specific projects intimately bound up with the experience and expertise of her staff. As a tough-minded administrator in a highly volatile field, she has developed a sensitivity to the merely faddish, and she is always careful to distinguish between what she calls the "rhetoric phase" and the "program phase" of each new challenge. If she can be said to have an operational philosophy, it is that the quicker a dispute over social priorities and moral principles can be reduced to the program level, the greater the chance for a satisfactory resolution. This philosophy was put to one of its most severe tests in recent years in a dispute over the control of an A.F.S.C. Field Office located in the heart of the black ghetto in Boston.

Every summer since 1952, the Peace Committee of the New England Regional Office had sponsored a retreat seminar known as the Avon Institute, devoted to the serious consideration—in an "unstructured" setting—of the basic issues of peace and war. The Institute was usually held at Geneva Point Camp, a privately operated campgrounds on the shore of Lake Winnipesaukee in New Hampshire, and was attended by several hundred members of the A.F.S.C. constituency in New England—white, liberal, middle-class, not necessarily Quaker but definitely oriented toward the Quaker approach to problem solving. The summer of 1967 brought some drastic changes in the Avon format. The brochure sent out to the regional mailing list promised

ON DOING GOOD

"The AVON INSTITUTE is going to be different this year." Instead of focusing on Vietnam or the arms race, the topic was going to be: "The Urban Crisis: Action Needed Now." Prospective conferees were assured that every effort had been made to ensure a challenging educational experience for all—"Discussion will be made more relevant and fruitful by the presence of many participants from the inner cities of New England where they are actively working for change." But other parts of the brochure struck an almost plaintively idyllic note:

> After lunch, talks on the background and relevance of Quakerism will be offered to all who are interested. Toward the end of the afternoon and after supper there will be lectures, panels or workshops with give-and-take from the floor encouraged. . . . The week at Avon will offer relaxation as well as the sharing of ideas. There will be time to swim in beautiful Lake Winnipesaukee, or to walk in the woods, or just to lie in the sun. Folk singing and dancing will enliven many evenings with a sense of fellowship.

What actually happened was that the Avon Institute on the Urban Crisis turned into a Black Power Crisis for the American Friends Service Committee. Any burgeoning sense of fellowship was permanently shattered on the second day when the thirty-three black adults at the Institute held a separate caucus and began drafting a manifesto that labeled the presence of white social agencies in black communities both "paternalistic and colonialistic." As a model for future relations between well-meaning whites and "an emerging black community," the manifesto called for a totally new status for the A.F.S.C. Field Office in the Roxbury section of Boston (the associate director of that office was among the signers). Specific demands included the creation of a "grass roots committee" in Roxbury with "full power for setting policy, fiscal autonomy, and authority to hire and fire

158

personnel"; the acceptance by the New England Regional Office of a policy of "buy Black and bank Black"; and the hiring of black males as directors of *all* A.F.S.C. field offices in black ghettos.

To the whites at Avon, the biggest shock was not the nature of the demands (97 of the 145 white attenders eventually endorsed them) but the fact that the blacks offered their manifesto on a take-it-or-leave-it basis. Although the word "nonnegotiable" had not yet entered the common vocabulary of crisis, it was clear that what the blacks were seeking was support *on their own terms* and not a dialogue leading to a new consensus.

The national office of the Community Relations Division was already well aware of the new mood of self-determination in the black community. Four A.F.S.C. observers had attended the National Conference on Black Power held in Newark that March. Their report had stressed the positive aspects of Black Power ("All this can be a healing process . . ."), while calmly noting that "there was general agreement on the failure of integration," "a strong feeling that the system is no good," and "the general tone . . . indicated that if violence was necessary to change the system, so be it." When the Community Relations Division moved to take up the demands of its own Black Power advocates, the tone of the discussion was set by Barbara Moffett in a memo to the division's executive committee: "One of the challenges is to sort out which demands run counter to our basic values and therefore cannot be met and which merely run counter to our habit and convenience." This sorting-out process, and the subsequent negotiations between the New England Regional Office and the newly formed Roxbury Community Committee, went on for more than a year. Before a decision was reached, the 1968 Avon Institute had come and gone in another un-Quakerly outburst of psycho- and sociodrama.

ON DOING GOOD

The announced theme this time was "Our Cities and Vietnam: A Search for Social Vision and Relevant Action," but as before, no one was in a mood to follow a prearranged script. Of the 325 participants, nearly a third were black, and a separate black caucus formed almost immediately. After several days of deliberation, the blacks decided to "seize" the building they had been meeting in (which happened to be the most comfortable living quarters on the campgrounds) as a symbol of the reparations owed to black people for their years of exploitation by a white racist society. Caught by surprise, the white participants fell into an acrimonious debate over the proper response to such "moral coercion." Eventually, it was decided *not* to call the police or close down the Institute, and the seizure of the building went unopposed, even though this meant the eviction of uninvolved third parties—including vacationing families with children. Then the blacks, who had initially warned "*All* white people not to approach within fifty feet of our new residence for *any* reason," returned to the Institute proper to present a demand for immediate and massive financial aid, with no strings attached, to black liberation groups in urban ghettos.

A number of white people, like Paul Goodman, one of the invited faculty members, had already left the camp in protest, accusing the Quaker leadership of selling out to the black militants and their white radical allies. At the final plenary session, those remaining voted overwhelmingly (by a show of hands) to endorse the demands of the black caucus. Stephen Cary, an associate executive secretary of the A.F.S.C., was one of the handful of dissenters. When asked to explain his dissent on the floor, he said that, speaking as a Quaker, it would be as much of a violation of his integrity to ask him to contribute money that might be used to buy guns, as it would be a vio-

160

lation of a black man's integrity to ask him to sit in the back of a bus.°

Meanwhile, the effort to move from "the rhetoric phase" to "the program phase" of the issues raised at the *previous* summer's Avon Institute had reached an impasse. The Service Committee had already met many of the original demands of the black caucus—such as the appointment of a black male to head the Roxbury Field Office, the acceptance of the locally organized Roxbury Community Committee as the "determiner" of A.F.S.C. program in the area, and the naming of several community leaders to the Personnel and Executive Committees of the New England Region. The sticking point was the demand that the Roxbury Field Office have complete autonomy in fiscal and personnel policy, while retaining the A.F.S.C. name and a share of the A.F.S.C. budget. It soon became apparent that not even the Service Committee was willing to bend its normal administrative procedures to that extent.

The Committee had originally gone into Roxbury in 1965 with what was supposed to be a five-year program aimed at housing inequities; at the end of that time, it was hoped that the work would "devolve" into community hands. Now, with two years to go on this timetable, the Community Relations Division suggested a greatly speeded-up transition period, during which the Service Committee would continue to pay all salaries, rent and other expenses (an estimated total of $46,000 a year) while com-

° Caught up in all these rhetorical cross-currents, thirty-three young children of the participants issued a manifesto of their own, which read in its entirety:

"To the parents of the Children of Geneva Point Camp. We the children of Geneva Point Camp think that it is unfair and unjust for the parents to decide to possibly end the conference for us children. We do not believe there is a difference between BLACKS and WHITES. We are all sisters and brothers."

munity leaders looked around for new sources of support. Even
this proposal, which would have preserved the Roxbury program's tax-exempt status and staff benefits like workmen's compensation, proved to be unacceptable to local pride and priorities. In the fall of 1968 the Roxbury Community Committee
became a separately incorporated entity known as the Roxbury
Action Program, and communication between Roxbury and the
New England Regional Office of the A.F.S.C. came to a virtual
halt. After much soul-searching, the Service Committee decided
that, welcome or not, it had a moral commitment to Boston's
black community at least through 1970—and it decided to
honor this commitment by donating $46,000 a year for the next
two years to the group that had inherited its field office. After
that, the Committee reserved the right to reconsider its support.

As far as Barbara Moffett was concerned, the failure to reach
a satisfactory consensus in the Roxbury negotiations was an un-
fortunate accident, having more to do with local conditions and
personality conflicts that with any basic inflexibility in A.F.S.C.
procedures. She cited the fact that almost all of the issues raised
in Roxbury had already been handled with a minimum of fuss
on the program level in other parts of the country. In several
Southern communities where the Service Committee had already established a relationship of mutual trust, funds were
being regularly channeled to independent black groups on a "no
strings" basis. In San Francisco, A.F.S.C. staff had contributed
indispensable skills to a grass-roots organization of welfare
mothers called GROUP, which had no formal connection with
the Service Committee and was therefore under no obligation to
observe Quaker guidelines concerning tactics and goals. In Chicago, black males were sought out to direct programs emanating
from the East Garfield Park Project House; the criterion was not
race *per se* but the demonstrably greater effectiveness, at this
moment in history, of local leaders who could live comfortably

in the area. (This distinction may sound sophistical to outsiders, but it is important to some members of the Committee, who argue that "black" and "local" are synonymous in East Garfield today only because of external pressures—a situation which is at least theoretically amenable to change.) The Committee had also sponsored social and cultural centers for American Indians in several large cities, where the responsibility for decision-making was divided between Service Committee representatives and leaders chosen from the community.

The executive secretary of the Community Relations Division has always relied on the ability of her staff to see through the rhetorical flourishes that sometimes masquerade as profound principles. "We always knew that the fight for civil rights wasn't just a matter of mixing bodies—at least I hope we did," she said. "Our experience with American Indians certainly taught us that people do better in unfamiliar surroundings when their own identity is clear; for instance, we know that Plains Indians, whose culture was shattered by the Indian Wars of the last century, have an even harder time adjusting to urban life than, say, an Indian from one of the Southwestern tribes. But this does *not* mean that we're going to agree to a policy change that says red people can only work with red people, black with black, brown with brown." She feels that the trouble with many inexperienced civil-rights leaders is that they let their guilt get the better of them, and become advocates for policies which they know are morally wrong and even detrimental to the interests of the minority groups involved. "We are not that new to the field, and we're not that concerned with our 'image.' Appealed to on conscience we're the most malleable of organizations; but bludgeoned by threats, we're the least." In practice, the Service Committee's response to both threats and appeals is usually determined by the recommendation of local staff people who are closest to the situation. But the discussion about the degree of

163

malleability proper to each case is carried on at a number of levels within the Committee structure.*

One member of the Community Relations Executive Committee, who was active in the fight to integrate the Washington, D.C., public schools several years before the 1954 Supreme Court decision, has often expressed the fear that the Committee is not being honest with black leaders. "Our sympathy for black people as victims is so great," she said, "that we go too far in blinding ourselves to their faults—we romanticize their strength and vitality. I'd be inclined to criticize their violent words and actions, and let the chips fall where they may. We made it a point of honor to challenge white violence and racism—we used so much ingenuity to show that you *could* have a black person working in the suburbs when we were *assured* you couldn't. . . . I only hope we use the same ingenuity to show the Black Power people that they can work with whites."

Another former staff member, a Negro woman who left the Committee to work for the N.A.A.C.P. Legal Defense and Education Fund, saw a very different danger in the tendency of certain Friends to congratulate themselves on their heroic past. She herself was brought up in the United Church of Christ, and was attracted to the Committee immediately after World War II because it offered the best opportunity at the time to bring a religious, nonviolent approach to bear on social issues. Although she has nothing but praise for the Committee's early involvement in the struggle against racial discrimination, she can re-

---

* When the Roxbury Action Program confronted the Service Committee in the fall of 1969 with an angrily worded "demand" for $350,000 to finance a housing rehabilitation project, the Community Relations Division calmly considered the project on its merits—and recommended that the Roxbury group be given $25,000 to explore more fully the feasibility of rehabilitating slum housing in Boston. This special grant—over and above the $46,000 already earmarked for Roxbury—was approved by the A.F.S.C. Board of Directors.

member her irritation at the fact that "many older Friends assumed that they were 'clear' on the race question because their grandfather had had a hand in the Underground Railroad or the Abolition Movement; they were unable to see that as middle-class white Americans, they have a part in perpetuating the structure of white racism today, no matter who their ancestors were. I used to chide my Quaker friends that they lacked a sense of Original Sin."

It is a fond hope of Bronson Clark, the executive secretary of the American Friends Service Committee, that the A.F.S.C. will find a "new relevancy" in the years ahead precisely because it is a "middle-class, white-dominated organization capable of interpreting black nationalism to middle-class whites." But Clark is painfully aware that there will be little progress toward meaningful social change at home until the war in Vietnam is ended. A convinced Friend, Clark is a burly, hard-driving man of fifty, with an aggressively outthrust jaw, who looks and talks like a successful Midwestern businessman—an identity he has assumed on occasion during the last two decades when not on a tour of duty with the Service Committee. Since World War II, when he was imprisoned for noncooperation with the draft law, he has alternated between a career as a corporation executive in his home state of Ohio and a career in international service that has taken him, among other places, to mainland China, with a Friends' ambulance unit, and to Morocco and Algeria, where he directed major relief programs. More recently, he coordinated the efforts of an eight-man working party on the booklet, "Peace in Vietnam," one of the A.F.S.C. publications that have provided fuel for an informed opposition to American policies in southeast Asia. In 1967, Clark resigned as vice-president of an optical-electronics firm in Oberlin to join the Service Committee's Special Vietnam Effort on a full-time basis. His selection as executive secretary in early 1968 coincided with a growing feeling among Committee members that the time had come to express the strongest possible collective witness against the war. The big question facing the leadership was whether to commit an act of corporate civil disobedience, for the first time in the Committee's half-century history, by knowingly violating a law of the United States.

Quakers have always tried to offer humanitarian aid to civilian sufferers on both sides of an armed conflict, and the Service Committee had acted according to this principle in the Spanish Civil War, the Chinese Civil War, and the Arab-Israeli wars among others. In Vietnam, the Committee's relief work had been concentrated in the southern provincial capital of Quang Ngai where an international staff operated a child day-care center and a hospital that specialized in prosthetics—making and fitting artificial limbs and training Vietnamese technicians to help care for the more than 40,000 civilian amputees in the South. But in the fall of 1966, in an effort to match this program— at least symbolically—with a program in the North, the Service Committee asked for and received permission from the State Department to ship $6,000 worth of medical supplies to Hanoi.

It is standard Committee policy to send qualified representatives along with such relief shipments, partly out of a desire to ensure efficient distribution, and partly out of a Quakerly distaste for faceless philanthropy ("The gift without the giver is cold"). But when the North Vietnamese refused entry to A.F.S.C. personnel, the Board of Directors decided to waive its usual requirement in this case, as an expression of the urgently felt need to establish some sort of contact with the people on the receiving end of American bombing raids. A few months later, the Johnson administration announced that all further requests for export licenses to North Vietnam would be denied, because there was no way of guaranteeing that the supplies were actually going to civilians and not to the Communist war effort. Almost immediately, several groups of concerned Quakers, including the New York Yearly Meeting of the Religious Society of Friends and an *ad hoc* committee calling itself simply A Quaker Action Group, informed the government that they intended to go on shipping medicines to North Vietnam *without* licenses, despite the fact that these shipments, arranged through the offices of the Canadian Friends Service Committee, would be in violation of the Trading with the Enemy Act. The government's response was to freeze the bank accounts of A Quaker Action Group, and to threaten legal proceedings against the individuals involved. The counter-response of A Quaker Action Group was to open new bank accounts (under the names of the threatened individuals) and to proceed with the shipments, including a dramatic voyage to Haiphong by the fifty-foot sailing vessel *Phoenix*. The announced intention of these actions was to demonstrate that no government had a right to regulate the humanitarian efforts of individuals to "heal and bind the wounds of war."

There were many people on the Service Committee who urged a similar policy of open defiance to the government's ruling. But there were also counsels of caution. Since the A.F.S.C. was hardly an *ad hoc* group, much more was involved than the assumption of personal risk by a handful of dedicated staff members. If the government froze the Committee's bank accounts, or cut off O.E.O. funds to certain programs, or took away the Committee's tax-exempt status, the health and well-being of large numbers of innocent third parties—from migrant workers in Florida and rent strikers in Chicago, to elderly people dependent on A.F.S.C. annuities and pensions—would be affected. Faced with an apparent conflict between two moral imperatives, the Committee typically paused to work out a new consensus.

167

ON DOING GOOD

Even before the change in the Johnson administration's policy, there had been a sense of uneasiness in the A.F.S.C. constituency about a humanitarian aid program that spent $250,000 in three years in the South and a token $6,000 in the North. In the fall of 1967, this uneasiness crystallized in a minute drafted by the Peace Committee of the New England Regional Office, which called on the Board to turn its entire Vietnam relief effort over to an international committee led by British and Canadian Friends, thereby freeing the A.F.S.C. to devote all its energy and funds to domestic programs aimed at "ending the war." The reasons given for this recommendation could not have been more frank: "The exploitation [of A.F.S.C. projects in Vietnam] by the American Government to improve its image and 'humanize' the war seems obvious. The cooperation that is necessary between A.F.S.C., the American military, and the Saigon regime to carry on our work there seems to legitimatize establishments we wholeheartedly abhor."

The reactions within the Service Committee to the New England minute were equally frank. Some people felt that it was not only morally justifiable, but *especially fitting,* for antiwar Americans to assist the victims of American bombs and shells. Another group thought that the Committee had to stay in Vietnam if only because an American Quaker presence would be of value to both sides once the fighting stopped and details of prisoner exchanges and similar delicate matters remained to be worked out. And there were many who simply believed that the task of rehabilitating amputees and caring for children was a "self-validating" act of love beyond all political considerations.

The moral ambiguities involved, and the passions that such an issue could arouse within the Committee, were a source of great concern to the then executive secretary, Colin Bell, who wrote: "To some, remaining in Vietnam appears to be too easy an accommodation with the military; to others, withdrawal appears as a too easy accommodation to the power of evil. I hope we will all recognize the deeply held convictions on every hand and in this time of anguish deal tenderly with each other."

In the spring of 1968, after nearly a year of corporate soul-searching (complicated by the process of selecting a new executive secretary), the Board of Directors reaffirmed the traditional Quaker policy of aiding civilian sufferers on both sides of the firing line. In practice, this meant continuing the work at Quang Ngai, while making a renewed effort to find a way to ship medical supplies to the North (or to areas controlled by the National Liberation Front in the South). Talks were initiated in Cambodia with representatives of the Hanoi government and the N.L.F. to determine what kind of aid was actually needed. Committee personnel had been in contact with the North Vietnamese and the Vietcong on a number of occasions during the preceding three years, to discuss issues ranging from the postwar reconstruction of the country to the release of a woman physician who had been captured in Hue during the Tet offensive while on leave from the A.F.S.C. center in Quang Ngai. (She was set free fifty-five days later, after the Vietcong ruefully explained that the soldiers who took her prisoner had no way of knowing she was associated with the Quakers.) Even with this background, and with the 1966 shipment as evidence of the Committee's good faith, it was not easy to overcome the suspicions of the Communist negotiators. The Communists kept telling the Quakers that if they really wanted to do some good, they should go home and work to end the war there; the A.F.S.C. representatives kept replying that the Committee was already extremely active along those lines, but that the maintenance of peaceful contacts between antagonists—such as the shipment of medical supplies—was in itself a step toward peace.

After several months of this kind of verbal sparring, an agreement was finally reached with the National Liberation Front, authorizing medical spokesmen for both sides to sit down and begin discussing specific aid requirements. Once the details were worked out in Cambodia, the Committee dutifully filed a new application for an export license in Washington. The date was September 10, 1968. A reply was requested within two weeks. A month later a State Department source informed the Committee that the government would have to say no if pressed for a reply at that time, but that the situation might be different in forty or fifty days. Reluctantly, the Committee decided that it was worth waiting a little longer if there was even an outside chance that the Johnson administration could be persuaded to change its mind again. (The Paris peace talks were in session, and it was assumed that the request for a delay had something to do with new developments on the diplomatic front.)

In the meantime, the Board of Directors asked Bronson Clark to conduct an extraordinary written poll of the entire staff and committee structure to make certain that there was a firm consensus in favor of shipping the drugs *without* government approval if necessary. The response was overwhelmingly favorable, although one regional executive committee and one national program committee reported "strong reservations" unless the shipment could be accompanied by A.F.S.C. spokesmen. (The National Liberation Front had already said that wartime conditions made it impossible for Committee personnel to enter the territory under its control.) Many of the respondents stressed the importance of making clear to all sides that the purpose of the shipment was humanitarian—with a basic religious motivation —and *not* political in any sense.

Three weeks before Christmas, the Board learned that the State Department had once again turned down its request for an export license. After a brisk discussion in which everyone present agreed that there was "unusual unity across the A.F.S.C. family" on this fateful step, the Board authorized the shipment

of $25,000 worth of procaine penicillin to civilian war sufferers
in areas of South Vietnam controlled by the National Liberation
Front. Of the three items that had been specifically requested by
the N.L.F., the Service Committee's medical expert had deemed
procaine penicillin the least likely to end up in battlefield use,
since it is a drug generally reserved for the treatment of second-
ary infections. (The N.L.F. representatives had been quite can-
did in admitting that as much as they would try to respect the
Quakers' wishes, there was no way to *guarantee* distribution to
civilians alone.) The penicillin was to be purchased abroad and
shipped in individual 10 cc. vials, together with disposable syringes. Each vial and each syringe was to be wrapped in a label
bearing a carefully worded inscription in both English and Vietnamese:

> The American Friends Service Committee (Quakers) gives med-
> ical aid to Vietnamese war sufferers in Quang Ngai. This gift is
> a similar expression of good will and friendship to the people of
> Vietnam from the American Friends Service Committee to help
> those civilians elsewhere in Vietnam who are suffering greatly
> because of the war.

Even greater care was taken with the wording of the explana-
tory statement to be released in this country. The effort to consider *all* the moral nuances of each issue, and to be fair to
everyone involved, has sometimes led members of the Service
Committee into a form of reasoning so conscientiously labyrin-
thine that it ends up losing the main thread. In announcing the
drug shipment, the Board and staff were especially anxious not
to do or say anything that might interfere, however slightly,
with the momentum of the Paris peace talks. In addition, no one
wanted to do anything to sour the Committee's relationship with
the State Department, which had remained amicable despite
major policy disagreements in the past. (The Board prizes its

ability to "speak truth to power" and get a sympathetic response.) Finally, no one wanted to say anything that might divert public attention to an issue which the Board considered strictly peripheral—its own precedent-breaking act of corporate civil disobedience.

In trying to strike a balance among all these considerations, Committee personnel drafted a statement which omitted *any* mention of the fact that the drugs were to be shipped without government approval. This startling omission was questioned by several members of the Board and staff, who felt that the Committee's obligation to be completely open with the public outweighed the otherwise admirable desire to adopt a nonprovocative posture in a confrontation with the government. (To try to shield the rest of the Committee's programs from the effects of possible government sanctions, a separate bank account had been designated to receive and disburse all funds connected with the drug shipment.) During the high-level discussion that followed, one of the most influential voices was that of Earle Edwards, the associate executive secretary for finance. He noted that the Board's decision happened to coincide with the year-end fund-raising drive. Given the controversial nature of the decision, it could be assumed that some contributors would want to sever their relation with the Committee when they learned of it; others might want to increase their support. In either case, Edwards expressed his concern that each contributor learn all about the decision as soon as possible from the Committee itself, so that no one would feel that his support was being solicited under false pretenses.

The statement ultimately approved by the Board was an almost perfect précis of the Service Committee's fundamental beliefs and attitudes, both in what it said and what it left unsaid. The complete text read as follows:

COMMUNITY

For more than three centuries, members of the Religious Society of Friends have borne witness to their belief in the sacredness of human personality. Life is precious to us because it is the gift of God and is to be used in His service. Therefore, we may not debase or exploit or crush it for any reason or in any circumstance. This has always been the Quaker witness to the world, and in our time the American Friends Service Committee has tried to remain faithful to it.

When the policies of power spill over into war, and men begin to hate and kill each other, the A.F.S.C. is concerned to relieve the suffering and to reconcile those who have been separated by conflict. And in places where prejudices, or the unconscious apathy of privilege, have operated to crush those who are poor or different, we have tried to offer help and to change the hearts and the institutions of the oppressor. To these ends we have worked with many branches of the family of man, whether American or European, African or Asian, Buddhist, Christian or Jew or Muslim. Sometimes our service has been among those whom other men call enemies, sometimes with those others call friends. They are all children of God, and we cannot let ourselves be separated from them by the arbitrary barriers that men build to rationalize their inhumanity.

This point of view, and the actions it leads to, are not always easy for our fellow citizens to accept, and we are encouraged by the loyal support that so many of you have given us for so long. Today we continue to need your support because our faith again calls us to aid those who are caught on the other side of the battle lines, this time in areas controlled by the National Liberation Front in Vietnam. We have long helped the Vietnamese who live in Saigon Government territory: in hospitals and orphanages, in a day-care center, in a prosthetics program for amputees in Quang Ngai and in the training of Buddhist social workers. Two years ago we contributed modest shipments of medical supplies to civilians on all sides of the conflict. We have now made the first of a series of shipments of procaine penicillin to civilian war sufferers in National Liberation Front areas, drawing upon funds specially raised for that purpose. At the same time we have sent a medical shipment of equal value to our Quaker service unit in Quang Ngai.

For years we have been developing and maintaining contact with all sides in this tragic war. As in all our other humanitarian efforts, we have acted with the knowledge of our government, and until now, within its regulations. We have met with NLF representatives in many places and on many occasions. We know something about their needs, even if the gulfs of history and culture still keep us from fully knowing them, or them from knowing us. These factors, and the terrible exigencies of war, have not yet made it possible for the NLF to permit A.F.S.C. representatives to accompany medical shipments beyond the point of their delivery into NLF hands. We regret this limitation, but we see our efforts as a continuum that we hope will lead to mutual growth of understanding and later personal participation. In the meantime, we have been promised and will expect reports on the use of our supplies for civilians and will continue to press for admission of A.F.S.C. personnel.

All of these considerations have been made known to our Government, and we have been in communication with its agencies for many months regarding our interest in sending help to civilians through an NLF agency charged with meeting civilian needs. We understand the reasons for the Administration's present unwillingness to approve such a step, but we still feel it right to proceed.

In taking this action, we earnestly believe that we are keeping faith with our Quaker commitment and with Jesus's parable of the Good Samaritan. This is our basic motivation. We are also concerned about prisoners of war—Americans held by the NLF, and Vietnamese held by American allies—and the contacts we have had with the NLF, and will continue to have through the medium of relief shipments, afford us the continuing opportunity to encourage the release of those who are im-

174

prisoned. It is important, too, for Americans to begin now to lay the foundation for future relationships with those on all sides of the Vietnam conflict. These must inevitably be established when the fighting stops, and the encouragement of private initiatives now may ease the way to greater understanding later. For these related reasons, but most of all as an expression of our religious concern, we have made this shipment, and intend to make others in the days ahead.

We ask your prayers that we may be rightly led in these matters.

By the time this statement was released to the press (on Dec. 18, 1968) and mailed to the entire A.F.S.C. constituency, officials in Saigon and Washington had been personally informed of the Board's action, and the first shipment of penicillin was already on its way.

The Associated Press picked up the story, but many newspapers (including *The New York Times*) ignored it entirely. Either the corporate prose style had proved impenetrable to the average city editor, or, as one member of the Committee's public relations department remarked: "Everyone probably assumed we've been doing this all along." Repercussions inside the A.F.S.C. family were limited to one resignation—a member of a program committee in the Youth Services Division—and a request from one staff member that his opposition to the shipment be noted in his personnel file. Within the larger Service Committee constituency, the reaction was of course harder to gauge, although Earle Edwards did not foresee any immediate net loss (or gain) in income, unless the government decided to apply legal sanctions.

As it turned out, the decision of the lame-duck Johnson administration was to turn the other cheek, or at least to shut both eyes, since no attempt was made to interfere with this or any subsequent shipment.* The following year, after the Nixon administration had taken office, the Service Committee applied for yet another export license, this time to send some $25,000 worth of medical equipment (for open-heart surgery) to the health ministry of North Vietnam. The arrangements had been worked out, in Hanoi, by Dr. Joseph Elder, a member of the A.F.S.C. Board of Directors, who had also persuaded the North Vietnamese to let him deliver the goods in person. Once again, the Committee was prepared to act without government approval. But on July 29, 1969, a license for the purchase of medical supplies abroad was granted by the U.S. Treasury Department, on the recommendation of the State Department, which had also validated Dr. Elder's passport for the trip to Hanoi. In a press release announcing the completed transaction, the Service Committee took note of the long-standing Quaker tradition of giving aid to all sides in a conflict situation, and cited, as an example, the earlier shipments of penicillin to the N.L.F.

To some people, the idea that any administration in Washington might decide to crack down on the Service Committee had always been faintly amusing. One knowledgeable but impartial observer prophesied: "The government will take on the American Friends Service Committee before it takes on the Roman Catholic Church—but only *just* before." For Gilbert White, however, the act of corporate civil disobedience was welcome proof that the moral concerns of individuals could still take precedence over a concern for the preservation of the institution itself. And for Bronson Clark, the entire sequence of events was

* When some of the syringes (with the A.F.S.C. labels still attached) were later found in Communist supply caches in Cambodia by invading American troops, the Committee offered no apology for the apparent diversion of its aid into military channels. In a brief statement Bronson Clark reiterated the humanitarian purpose of the shipment and underscored the fact that the U.S. government had been kept fully informed of A.F.S.C. intentions and actions in this area.

an indication that the Service Committee could continue to play the role of "friend and critic" to the American government even while strenuously opposing many of its policies. "People have a feeling that our society is coming apart at the hinges," Clark said at the time. "We've lost confidence, we're unable to organize to do the things we know we have to do; we can't seem to break out of the past. What the Committee has done is very encouraging. It's fantastic in a way that a fifty-year-old organization with thousands of contributors and hundreds of staff people is not so encrusted with barnacles that it can't reach a consensus on a step like this. I have a feeling that in the next few years we're going to be much used by men of good will, in government and elsewhere, as a link to the great reservoir of liberal values in this country."

DATE DUE

MAR 2 1999	

GAYLORD   PRINTED IN U.S.A.